Dreams of
Love and Power

DREAMS OF LOVE AND POWER

On Shakespeare's Plays

JOSEPH H. SUMMERS

CLARENDON PRESS · OXFORD

1984

Oxford University Press, Walton Street, Oxford OX2 6DP
London New York Toronto
Delhi Bombay Calcutta Madras Karachi
Kuala Lumpur Singapore Hong Kong Tokyo
Nairobi Dar es Salaam Cape Town
Melbourne Auckland

and associated companies in
Beirut Berlin Ibadan Mexico City Nicosia

Oxford is a trade mark of Oxford University Press

Published in the United States
by Oxford University Press, New York

British Library Cataloguing in Publication Data
Summers, Joseph H.
Dreams of love and power : on Shakespeare's
plays.
1. Shakespeare, William—Knowledge—
Psychology   2. Dreams in literature
I. Title
822.3'3   PR3069.D67
ISBN 0-19-812823-1

Library of Congress Cataloging in Publication Data
Summers, Joseph H. (Joseph Holmes), 1920-
Dreams of love and power
Includes index.
1. Shakespeare, William, 1564-1616—Criticism and
interpretation—
Addresses, essays, lectures.
2. Shakespeare, William, 1564-1616—Dramatic production—
Addresses, essays, lectures. I. Title.
PR2976.S777   1984   822.3'3   84-9526
ISBN 0-19-812823-1

Typeset by DMB (Typesetting), Oxford
and printed in Great Britain
at the University Press, Oxford
by David Stanford
Printer to the University

For
Mary,
Hazel,
and
Joseph

Preface

I first taught an introductory course on the plays of Shakespeare during my first year of full-time teaching in 1948-9; except when I have been on leave, I have taught such a course almost every year since. All the essays here derive from the experience of continually trying to understand with a class what goes on in Shakespeare's plays. In the process I have come to believe that nearly all the plays share a primary concern with the desires, hopes, fears—the dreams—of the dramatic characters, and that to a large extent we become intimately engaged in the dramas as we perceive the relations between those 'dreams' and our own desires, hopes, and fears, both as an audience in the theatre (however imaginary) and as actors off-stage.

These essays began, however, not as attempts to illustrate any theory but as efforts to solve (or at least to understand) specific problems which have come up in class or at performances in the theatre: how can actors play Act I, scene ii of *The Tempest* convincingly? what are we to make of *Antony and Cleopatra*, Act III, scene xiii? what about the ending of *Measure for Measure*? The ideas for the essays have developed gradually, but the actual writing has come chiefly in response to special occasions and to breaks from teaching duties during the past ten years. Versions of both 'The Anger of Prospero' and the essay on *Antony and Cleopatra* were delivered as lectures at the University of Kent while I was teaching there in 1972. The first drafts of the essays on *King Lear* and *Measure for Measure* were written while I enjoyed a fellowship at the Folger Shakespeare Library in 1976. The essays on *A Midsummer Night's Dream*, *The Winter's Tale*, and *Hamlet* were begun and substantially completed while I was in residence at the Huntington Library in 1980-1. Earlier versions of two chapters have appeared previously: 'The Anger of Prospero' in a special issue of the *Michigan Quarterly Review* (1973) in honour of Frank Huntley, and ' "Look there, look there!": The Ending of *King Lear*' in *English Renaissance Studies Presented to Dame Helen Gardner in honour of her Seventieth Birthday* (Oxford, 1980).

I am grateful to the University of Rochester for generous

academic leaves of absence and for such colleagues as Cyrus Hoy, Russ McDonald, David Richman, David Samuelson, and Stephen Wigler, who have helped with specific criticisms; to the Folger Shakespeare Library, the National Endowment for the Humanities, and the Huntington Library for fellowships and facilities which made the writing pleasant as well as possible; and to the readers of the Oxford University Press for helpful criticisms and suggestions. That I was finally able to complete the book is surely owing in part to the astonishingly congenial and stimulating group of scholars concerned with the Renaissance by whom I was surrounded at the Huntington Library in 1980-1, including A. R. Braunmuller, Leland Carlson, Elizabeth and Daniel Donno, Madeleine Doran, R. A. Foakes, French Fogle, Charles Forker, Roland Frye, Christopher Grose, S. K. Heninger, Geneva Phillips, Jonathan Post, James Riddell, William Ringler, Alexander Shurbanov, Hallett Smith, Susan Snyder, John Steadman, Stanley Stewart, James Thorpe, Edward Weismiller, and George Walton Williams. Such a group made work a delight.

JOSEPH H. SUMMERS

The University of Rochester

Contents

Note

All the quotations from Shakespeare are taken from the New Arden editions unless some other edition is specifically cited. The only substantial departure from the Arden texts is that speech-prefixes are always given in full.

I

Dreams of Love and Power:
A Midsummer Night's Dream

Most of the critics and scholars who have written about *A Midsummer Night's Dream* in recent years have united to praise it: a great many of them love it. Frank Kermode considered it 'Shakespeare's best comedy'.[1] F. P. Wilson remarked, 'The play mingles theme after theme in what (not to speak extravagantly) is a miracle of construction.'[2] Although almost everyone who writes on the play remembers uneasily Bottom's 'Man is but an ass if he go about to expound this dream' (IV. i. 205-6),[3] the temptations both to expound and to speak extravagantly seem almost irresistible. Moreover, the popular recent productions of the play by Peter Brook, Peter Hall, and many others, in the theatre, the cinema, and the opera-house (Benjamin Britten's *A Midsummer Night's Dream* is surely a masterpiece) give welcome evidence that contemporary enjoyment and even love of the play are not merely scholarly or academic phenomena. We have come a long way from Pepys's remark of 29 September 1662, 'It is the most insipid ridiculous play that ever I saw in my life.'[4]

Readers not only delight in the play, but have come to see it as central to Shakespeare's achievement. Harold F. Brooks, in his splendidly comprehensive New Arden edition, describes it as making triumphant use of various devices of plot, construction, characterization, and theme from the earlier *Comedy of Errors*, *Two Gentlemen of Verona*, and *Love's Labour's Lost*, and he believes that Sly's dream in *The Taming of the Shrew* anticipates

[1] 'The Mature Comedies', *Early Shakespeare*, Stratford-upon-Avon Studies, 3, ed. John Russell Brown and Bernard Harris (London, 1961), p. 214.

[2] 'Shakespeare's Comedies', *Shakespearian and Other Studies*, ed. Helen Gardner (Oxford, 1969), p. 78. In 'The Moon and the Fairies in *A Midsummer Night's Dream*', *University of Toronto Quarterly*, 24 (1955), 234-46, Ernest Schanzer gave a thorough analysis of the play's structure.

[3] I quote throughout from the Arden edition of Harold F. Brooks (London, 1979).

[4] Quoted by Brooks, p. x, from *Diary*, ed. R. C. Latham and W. Matthews, iii. 208; in view of the number of revivals (in however butchered forms), Pepys's response seems to have been unusual even in his time.

significantly Bottom's dream; he also reminds us that it was in
the *Shrew* we first heard of 'the effect of love in idleness'.[5] After
quoting Croce as considering the play the 'quintessence' of the
comedies as *Hamlet* is of the tragedies, F. P. Wilson remarked
that *A Midsummer Night's Dream* initiated the 'run of five comedies' (with *The Merchant of Venice, Much Ado About Nothing, As
You Like It,* and *Twelfth Night*) that 'has kept its popularity upon
the stage almost without a break from Shakespeare's day to
ours.'[6] Brooks judges that 'Both in form and feeling, *A Midsummer Night's Dream* is the most lyrical of all Shakespeare's plays',
and he sees it as climactic to the three earlier lyrical plays of the
mid-1590s: *Love's Labour's Lost, Richard II,* and *Romeo and Juliet.*[7]
A number of readers have recognized in Bottom a lowly
ancestor of Falstaff, and almost everyone who writes about the
play comments on its anticipations of the music and magic of
The Tempest. In his fine study, *Something of Great Constancy: The
Art of 'A Midsummer Night's Dream'*, David Young suggested
that the playwright seemed conscious of the centrality of the
play: 'The amalgam of styles and means indicates a conviction
that the key to improvement was *inclusiveness*, the wedding of

---

[5] Brooks, pp. lxxvi-lxxxii. The passage in *The Taming of the Shrew* reads as follows:

Tranio. I pray, sir, tell me, is it possible
That love should of a sudden take such hold?
Lucentio. O Tranio, till I found it to be true,
I never thought it possible or likely.
But see, while idly I stood looking on,
I found the effect of love in idleness,
And now in plainness do confess to thee,
That art to me as secret and as dear
As Anna to the Queen of Carthage was,
Tranio, I burn, I pine, I perish, Tranio,
If I achieve not this young modest girl.
(I. i. 146-56)

[6] *Shakespearian and Other Studies,* p. 72.

[7] Arden edition, pp. li, xlii-xliv. The order of composition of *Romeo and Juliet* and
A Midsummer Night's Dream is not surely known, but Brooks sides with most recent
scholars in considering the *Dream* probably the later play. I find it almost impossible to
believe that Shakespeare could have written *Romeo and Juliet,* IV. v., with its lines such
as the Nurse's 'She's dead, deceas'd! She's dead! Alack the day!' (23), Lady Capulet's
response, 'Alack the day! She's dead, she's dead, she's dead!' (24), and the Nurse's
later 'O day, O day, O day, O hateful day' (52) *after* he had written *A Midsummer
Night's Dream,* V. i, with its parody of such expressions of grief in Pyramus's

O grim-look'd night! O night with hue so black!
O night, which ever art when day is not!
O night, O night, alack, alack, alack . . .
(168-70)

elements previously considered incompatible.'[8]

The play's title announces much of what we may expect: it concerns a dream or dreams (or even *is* a dream?) proper for midsummer night, the shortest night of the year, traditionally associated with festival, fertility, and erotic abandon.[9] This dream presents love in an astonishing number of kinds or forms— as fantasy or illusion, infatuation, obsession, torment, enchantment, misunderstood convention, dotage, pursuit or chase, game, conflict or battle, reconciliation, discovery, awakening, celebration, joy, sanity, reality: 'inclusiveness' indeed seems intended and achieved. And just as love comes to seem almost impossibly multifarious in its forms and meanings and effects, so 'dream', too, proliferates to include the literal dreams—of desire or fear, reconciliation or delusion—of someone asleep; the waking imagination's individual dreams of loss or desire or fulfilment; the dreams or 'shadows' of poetic or dramatic creations presented on the stage or recollected in the mind; and the collective dream of human life.

It is astonishing that a play that attempts to say so much should manage to say anything at all: conscious attempts to include (not to say attempt to reconcile) the usual antinomies of human life frequently result in something like an attempt to meditate on the transcendental 'Oom' which, however profound in philosophical terms, fails to communicate very much on stage. Shakespeare solved the problems dramatically not only by creating such contrasting groups of characters (Theseus, Hippolyta, and their court; the lovers; Bottom and his crew; the fairies and Puck), but particularly by creating a shifting sequence of movements of language, verse, tone, and action, within as well as between scenes, that continually surprise and delight us.

As we respond to those movements, we are forced repeatedly to shift our perspectives—frequently when we have barely achieved them. In his opening lines Theseus introduces the moonlight which drenches the play, but his impatience for the

[8] New Haven and London, 1966, p. 33. I am also indebted to G. K. Hunter's *William Shakespeare: The Late Comedies* (London, 1962).

[9] See C. L. Barber's 'May Games and Metamorphosis on a Midsummer Night', *Shakespeare's Festive Comedy* (Princeton, 1959), pp. 119-62; cf. Brooks, Arden edition, pp. lxix-lxx.

new moon and his wedding cuts through the romantic feeling:

> but O, methinks, how slow
> This old moon wanes! She lingers my desires,
> Like to a step-dame or a dowager
> Long withering out a young man's revenue.   (I. i. 3-6)

However shocking in another context, the notion that young men yearn for the early deaths of their stepmothers, grandmothers, or even mothers when they stand between them and the full enjoyment of their inheritances, is presented here as if it were normal and even ruefully amusing, since it is compared to the unquestionably sympathetic impatience of a bridegroom for his wedding night. Hippolyta firmly establishes a mood of romance with 'Four days will quickly steep themselves in night; / Four nights will quickly dream away the time . . .' (7-8), but it is roughly broken by the entrance of the irate Egeus, with melodramatic charges and demands for either his daughter's obedience or her death. The tone modulates to something like that of a judicial procedure as Theseus hears the charges and begins to investigate them, but there continue to be odd shifts or expansions. Theseus dilates on the single alternative to death ('to abjure / For ever the society of men') if Hermia persists in disobedience to her father's choice of Demetrius as her husband:

> Therefore, fair Hermia, question your desires,
> Know of your youth, examine well your blood.
> Whether, if you yield not to your father's choice,
> You can endure the livery of a nun,
> For aye to be in shady cloister mew'd,
> To live a barren sister all your life,
> Chanting faint hymns to the cold fruitless moon.
>
> (67-73)

The poignance is unmistakable, as is the fact that within the action of this play a life of virginity will be viewed as unmitigated, 'fruitless' disaster to be avoided at almost any cost.[10]

---

[10] Both Hallett Smith and Russ McDonald have questioned my formulation here, and Harold F. Brooks (Arden edition, pp. cxxxi-cxxxii) argues strongly the opposite case: 'The honouring of marriage is worth more from a dramatist who is aware of an alternative ideal, and pays it no less honour. The myth of the imperial votaress is not solely a compliment to the Virgin Queen, and a means of giving importance to the "little western flower": it is an organic part of the marriage theme. The freely chosen virginity it exalts is, moreover, in contrast with the virginity to be enforced, if

If we have had any serious doubts about the direction of this play (or fears that the dreams would be primarily within the realm of nightmare), they are quickly put to rest. Immediately after Theseus's determination of the three alternatives, Demetrius pleads to his would-be mistress and rival:

> Relent, sweet Hermia; and Lysander, yield
> Thy crazed title to my certain right. (91-2)

And Lysander's reply *is* rather crazy in a sense Demetrius never intended: wonderfully unexpected and very funny:

> You have her father's love, Demetrius:
> Let me have Hermia's; do you marry him.
> (93-4)

If the initial promise that the action will end with a wedding has not been sufficient, these lines reassure us that this play is a comedy, and that nothing fatal, irreparable, or unforgivable will occur to disturb our pleasure and our laughter.

The shifts continue throughout the play and continually surprise us. Some things that give extra tension or anticipation to the surprises can be overlooked in a private reading of the play but are almost inescapable in a performance. From the moment when we enter the woods at the beginning of Act II until Act IV, scene i, lines 101f., when Puck, Oberon, and Titania leave, we see continuously a stage on which supernatural beings are either actors, directors, observers, or dreaming potential participants; even less than with ordinary dramatic characters can we know what these beings, usually invisible to the others on stage, may do or say. All the actions are rendered more problematic still by the fact that from just before the lovers enter the woods at Act II, scene ii, until the end of Act IV, scene i, when Bottom awakes and returns to Athens, more than half of the lines are spoken on a stage containing one or more characters asleep (at one point there are six of them), supposedly dream-

---

Theseus' sentence stands, upon Hermia. To find place for a noble virginity in his marriage-play must have been deeply satisfying to Shakespeare's "comprehensive soul".' But Oberon's graceful speech (II. i. 155-72) precisely contrasts the semi-divine powers of the 'throned' vestal virgin who defeated Cupid's 'fiery shaft' with the condition of every creature, mortal, immortal, or legendary, within this play. The obeisance to values above love and marriage was almost obligatory in Elizabethan England—particularly in a play that might possibly be performed before the Queen. But the preservation of virginity is not a conceivable possibility for the central characters within a Shakespearian comedy.

ing, almost surely to awaken to a radically changed inner conviction of love or to a radically changed loved one, or, as Bottom does, to an entirely changed world. Long before Puck's epilogue, the fairies and those dreaming figures have cast doubts on the complex relationships between reality, the play, and the dream.

As the action proceeds, we can almost anticipate when the brief slumbers of Demetrius and Lysander will be disturbed, for the movements of the lovers are patterned nearly mathematically. But from the moments when Titania's attendants sing her lullaby (II. ii. 9-23) and immediately thereafter Oberon squeezes the juice of love-in-idleness on her eyelids (26-33), the sleeping figure of Titania makes for increasing tension as we wait for her to wake on that noisy and often crowded stage. In his charm, Oberon has mentioned the possibility that she may first see an animal, and he has ended it with 'Wake when some vile thing is near' (33). From the point of view of royal fairies, however, almost any of the ordinary human beings might qualify as 'vile'. Could it possibly be the loving Lysander or Hermia who appear immediately? the unnaturally pursuing Helena or the unnaturally fleeing Demetrius? Bottom or Quince —or even Snug, Flute, Snout, or Starveling—as they first plan for, and then begin, their rehearsal? We wait with increasing expectations and then Bottom, marvellously transformed with the ass's head, enters, and we *know* that he must be the anticipated vile thing, more amusingly 'animal' than we could possibly have predicted. But the expected moment is further delayed as Quince shouts, all the others run off, and then, under Puck's driving pursuit, first Snout runs on and off stage again, and then Quince does the same—both loudly exclamatory. It is only with the first quatrain of Bottom's song that Titania awakes: 'What angel wakes me from my flowery bed?' And Bottom, either not hearing or not noticing her (or perhaps not wishing to, or not wishing to leave his song, the antidote to his fear, unfinished) does not answer, but sings his second quatrain— and comments on it:

> *The finch, the sparrow, and the lark,*
> *The plain-song cuckoo gray,*
> *Whose note full many a man doth mark,*
> *And dares not answer nay—*

for indeed, who would set his wit to so foolish a bird? Who would give
a bird the lie, though he cry 'cuckoo' never so?   (III. i. 125-31)

Who would reply to the queen of the fairies unless he were
addressed directly and unmistakably? Is he sure that he is
awake? Are we? More than any earlier Shakespeare play, *A
Midsummer Night's Dream* demonstrates the exuberance of a
playwright who has mastered his craft so surely that he can joyfully put it to new uses—play with it and with his audience.

The playing, of course, proceeds upon the assumption that
the audience will enjoy the game. A number of Shakespeare's
plays might have been entitled or subtitled 'As You Like It' or
'What You Will'—and not just the comedies. The evidence
suggests that in most of the plays Shakespeare intended to
please the playgoers, not merely for the usual financial reasons,
but for the profound reason, too, that the best literature inevitably gives pleasure as it reflects and gives shape and meaning
to our experiences, our dreams, and our desires. The comedies
always move towards weddings and celebrations; they characteristically end with lovers taking their places in a newly recon-
stituted adult world; and whatever contemporary moralists or
theologians had to say about love, the plays' happy endings are
associated with the triumph of love rather than of reason, discipline, or parental, civil, or ecclesiastical authority. Love, or
what appears to be love, is also, of course, a dangerous and
potentially destructive force; it frequently entails sorrow and it
can lead to disaster and death. But it is inevitably involved in
the process of growing up successfully—the achieving of a state
in which one can imagine and even desire the existence of
another individual in his own right and not merely as an
appendage or reflection of oneself. Despite all the advice of the
moralists, there is no sure rule or formulaic way through or
around the confusions, the problems, and the traps. If we
laugh at the plays (and *want* to laugh), it is partly because we
recognize that few human beings ever achieve a desirable state
of love without either behaving, or appearing to behave, foolishly. The most fundamentally absurd image of all of Shakespeare's lovers is that of the man madly in love who claims and
believes that he is acting rationally. Lysander here gives it
classic expression. After he has vowed eternal love to Hermia
('And then end life when I end loyalty!'—II. ii. 62), he falls

asleep, his eyes are anointed with 'love-in-idleness' by Puck, and he awakes to see Helena and falls insanely in love with her. The fickleness of his emotions and sexual desires is only matched by the absoluteness of his rhetorical commitments. But our laughter is aroused chiefly by his insistence that his decision is totally rational and a natural result of his maturation:

> Not Hermia, but Helena I love:
> Who will not change a raven for a dove?
> The will of man is by his reason sway'd,
> And reason says you are the worthier maid.
> Things growing are not ripe until their season:
> So I, being young, till now ripe not to reason;
> And, touching now the point of human skill,
> Reason becomes the marshal to my will,
> And leads me to your eyes, where I o'erlook
> Love's stories, written in love's richest book.
>
> (II. ii. 112-21)

No one was ever 'completely rational' when he 'fell in love': the phrases are self-contradictory. It is hardly rational in a larger sense, however (it is certainly inhuman), to attempt to live, or even to desire, a life of completely rational control, totally opposed to, or oblivious of, the emotions and the senses, the love of others or another. But however desirable love is, to abandon all notions of reason or to attempt to live apart from reason may invite destruction. The problems are congruent with human life. A particular problem within romantic comedy is how the audience can be moved from initial laughter at the absurdities of young lovers to joyful acceptance of the union of those lovers as a happy ending, the absurdities somehow forgotten, accepted, corrected, or transcended. *A Midsummer Night's Dream* differs from most of the comedies in the degree to which its four groups of characters function on differing metaphysical and social levels, as well as have differing conceptions and experiences of romantic love. The absurd young lovers here are placed within a framework both temporal and critical.

We begin with Theseus and Hippolyta. For them the 'Boy-Meets-Girl era of mirrors and muddle'[11] is over. Theseus's past, according to the legends both we and Oberon remember,

---

[11] W. H. Auden, 'Mundus et Infans', *Collected Poems*, ed. Edward Mendelson (London, 1976), p. 252.

has included a lurid variety of acts of unfaithfulness and sexual aggression—the rapes or betrayals of Perigouna, 'Aegles', Ariadne, and Antiopa, among others (II. i. 78-80); and Titania, with less legendary justification, charges that the 'bouncing Amazon' Hippolyta was formerly Oberon's 'buskin'd mistress' and 'warrior love' (II. i. 70-1). But we are not concerned with any of that at the beginning of the play: those affairs and the courtship which gave mythic form to the entire battle between the sexes, the war between the Athenians and the Amazons, are now past. Theseus and Hippolyta are lovers who have 'come through'. They are royal figures who now firmly love and accept each other's love, impatiently await the wedding that will signal the public recognition of their union, and fill the intervening time with celebration.

> *Theseus.* Hippolyta, I woo'd thee with my sword,
> And won thy love doing thee injuries;
> But I will wed thee in another key,
> With pomp, with triumph and with revelling.
>
> (I. i. 16-19)

In Oberon and Titania, whom we meet in Act II, the ordinary problems of a long-married couple are both exaggerated in their jealousies, infidelities, obsessions (sexual or procedural—with page-boys or lovers), and struggles for power, and also distanced by their status (both royal and immortal) and by laughter. Their quarrels are hardly felt as threats to the love and happiness that Theseus and Hippolyta await or that the lovers so frantically pursue: instead, Titania, in one of Shakespeare's loveliest Ovidian inventions, identifies them as a source of all the 'unnatural' disorders of Nature herself:

> These are the forgeries of jealousy:
> . . .
> . . . with thy brawls thou hast disturb'd our sport.
> Therefore the winds, piping to us in vain,
> As in revenge have suck'd up from the sea
> Contagious fogs; which, falling in the land,
> Hath every pelting river made so proud
> That they have overborne their continents.
> The ox hath therefore stretch'd his yoke in vain,
> The ploughman lost his sweat, and the green corn

Hath rotted ere his youth attain'd a beard;
The fold stands empty in the drowned field,
And crows are fatted with the murrion flock;
The nine-men's-morris is fill'd up with mud,
And the quaint mazes in the wanton green
For lack of tread are undistinguishable.
The human mortals want their winter cheer:
No night is now with hymn or carol blest.
Therefore the moon, the governess of floods,
Pale in her anger, washes all the air,
That rheumatic diseases do abound.
And thorough this distemperature we see
The seasons alter: hoary-headed frosts
Fall in the fresh lap of the crimson rose;
And on old Hiems' thin and icy crown,
An odorous chaplet of sweet summer buds
Is, as in mockery, set . . .

. . .

And this same progeny of evils comes
From our debate, from our dissension;
We are their parents and original.

(II. i. 81-117)

That passage may suggest the paradox of tragedy in little: in content it concerns loss, disorder, decay, the destruction of beauty, disease, and death; but we attend its 'imitation' with fascination and delight in its beauty. With the application of love-in-idleness, the married Titania can become as madly sexually obsessed as any of the younger lovers—and even more absurdly so. But when Dian's bud releases her from the enchantment, she wakes as from a dream that was a nightmare ('My Oberon! What visions have I seen! / Methought I was enamour'd of an ass.'—IV. i. 75-6); reconciled with Oberon, she is ready to dance with him again and to join in the blessings of the bridal beds.

The notions of Bottom and his crew about romantic love are as crudely naïve as their notions about dramatic conventions: both love and drama are exotic, utterly alien, forms or feelings divorced from their own daily concerns; neither, according to their imaginations, has any relationship with probability, and for neither must language necessarily make parsable sense.

Quince either thinks or diplomatically pretends to think that

Bottom will make a likely dramatic lover (I. ii. 79-82). [12] But although Bottom would happily take on all the standard dramatic roles and eventually accepts a role as a tragic lover with some enthusiasm ('That will ask some tears in the true performing of it. If I do it, let the audience look to their eyes: I will move storms, I will condole in some measure'—21-3), he would prefer that of a tyrant: 'I could play Ercles rarely, or a part to tear a cat in, to make all split' (24-6). The crew's ludicrous version of Pyramus and Thisbe, lovers fated like Romeo and Juliet, who find only death when they flee from opposing parental authority, distances the young Athenian lovers who have also fled to the woods even more decisively from tragic possibilities than Titania's and Oberon's metaphysical discord and reachieved harmony distance them from the possibilities of ordinary sour marriages.

But when, quite unexpectedly, Bottom is suddenly physically transformed and, equally suddenly, finds himself selected as a love object by a passionately enchanted Fairy Queen, he hangs on to his sense of reality and remains endearingly unflappable.

> *Titania.* I pray thee, gentle mortal, sing again:
> Mine ear is much enamour'd of thy note;
> So is mine eye enthralled to thy shape;
> And thy fair virtue's force perforce doth move me
> On the first view to say, to swear, I love thee.

Bottom. Methinks, mistress, you should have little reason for that. And yet, to say the truth, reason and love keep little company together nowadays. The more the pity that some honest neighbours will not make them friends. Nay, I can gleek upon occasion.

> (III. i. 132-41)

As almost every audience recognizes, the scenes between Bottom and Titania do not descend to nightmarish bestiality, [13] but

---

[12] Quince's remarks when he thinks the play will not go on because of Bottom's disappearance suggest it is no pretence:

Quince. You have not a man in all Athens able to discharge Pyramus but he.
Flute. No, he hath simply the best wit of any handicraft man in Athens.
Quince. Yea, and the best person too; and he is a very paramour for a sweet voice.
                                                                    (IV. ii. 7-12)

[13] Contrast Jan Kott, 'Titania and the Ass's Head', *Shakespeare Our Contemporary* (Garden City, NY, 1966), pp. 213-36.

are extremely funny. Bottom is not transformed into either a physical or an emblematic ass; he is only provided, temporarily, with an ass's head. The text seems also clearly to indicate that, when faced with what seems the complete fulfilment of a traditional (and perhaps ultimate) male fantasy of 'love-in-idleness'—being specially chosen as a lover by a beautiful and passionately willing Queen of the Faeries—*this* mortal is interested only in oats, hay, having his ears scratched, braying bad songs, and giving orders and making bad jokes to the servants. Bottom seems as far from understanding or responding to physical sexuality—at least in this context—as he is from understanding the conventions of romantic love or the drama. He is so absurd that Titania only seems able to keep herself from waking from her enchantment by having him muzzled:

> Tie up my love's tongue, bring him silently.   (III. i. 194)

Her unsuccessful attempt to seduce the sleepy, ass-headed Bottom is the climax of the night's frustrations and unnatural reversals, in which women pursue men—unavailingly.

Although Hermia and Helena remain fixed in their original romantic attachments (not the only time the plays suggest that women may be less fickle than men), all the young lovers seem victims of love-in-idleness even before Puck begins to anoint sleeping eyes. Their loves are fanciful, obsessive, and untested. Helena's seems also hopelessly unreciprocated: Demetrius had courted her, made her 'devoutly' dote, and then abandoned her for *his* new unrequited love, Hermia (I. i. 107-9). And the lovers are moonily literary: Hermia and Lysander enjoy meditating on the notion that 'The course of true love never did run smooth';

> But either it was different in blood—
> *Hermia.* O cross! too high to be enthrall'd to low.
> *Lysander.* Or else misgraffed in respect of years—
> *Hermia.* O spite! too old to be engag'd to young.
> *Lysander.* Or else it stood upon the choice of friends—
> *Hermia.* O hell! to choose love by another's eyes.
> *Lysander.* Or, if there were a sympathy in choice,
> War, death, or sickness did lay siege to it,
> Making it momentany as a sound,
> Swift as a shadow, short as any dream,

> Brief as the lightning in the collied night,
> That, in a spleen, unfolds both heaven and earth,
> And, ere a man hath power to say 'Behold!',
> The jaws of darkness do devour it up:
> So quick bright things come to confusion.
>
> (I. i. 134-49)

It is surely no accident that not one of their exemplary cases is at all close to their own relatively commonplace situation of lovers whose union is barred simply by parental opposition (however complicated and intensified by peculiar laws), and that every one of them implies serious barriers to fulfilment if not sudden and tragic separation and death: the situations of these legendarily frustrated lovers are all so much more *interesting* than the alternative of simply getting married and living more-or-less happily afterwards. The lovely recollection of *Romeo and Juliet* at the end of Lysander's speech is surely proper for this charming, untried pair: they find the possibility of being glamorous, tragic lovers like Romeo and Juliet—or perhaps like Pyramus and Thisbe—in some ways admirable and titillating. They plan a romantic elopement to the woods by moonlight, imagining a dramatic climax of their love quite removed from the ordinary social and familial worlds that they know.[14]

Helena plays her role of the abandoned, abjectly pursuing damsel to the hilt. Instead of welcoming the elopement of Hermia with Lysander as the elimination of her rival for Demetrius's affections, she betrays it to him, knowing that she is behaving foolishly, just for another sentimental glimpse of her lover:

> and for this intelligence
> If I have thanks, it is a dear expense.
> But herein mean I to enrich my pain,
> To have his sight thither and back again.   (I. i. 248-51)

Later, she grovels passionately:

> I am your spaniel; and Demetrius,
> The more you beat me, I will fawn on you.

---

[14] It is interesting, though, that Shakespeare's gentlemen frequently retain some realistic prudence despite romantic intoxication: Lysander plans to flee to a 'widow aunt, a dowager / Of great revenue, and she hath no child— / From Athens is her house remote seven leagues— / And she respects me as her only son' (I. i. 157-60): the house is outside the legal jurisdiction of Athens and Lysander thinks he stands a good chance of inheriting.

> Use me but as your spaniel, spurn me, strike me,
> Neglect me, lose me; only give me leave,
> Unworthy as I am, to follow you.   (II. i. 203-7)

As everyone knows, spaniels that behave in this fashion are more frequently kicked out of the way than beaten. It is possible to admire Demetrius's restraint (while laughing at his ineffectualness) when he replies:

> Tempt not too much the hatred of my spirit;
> For I am sick when I do look on thee.
>   (II. i. 211-12)

We must laugh when he attempts to frighten her with a hint that he might harm or even rape her—an obvious impossibility under the circumstances. Finally, he can only run.

Demetrius here, like the Lysander who later exclaims, 'Away, you Ethiope!' to his brunette former love (III. ii. 257), exemplifies the usual assumption of the victim of love-in-idleness that he possesses the right, if not the duty, to say and do exactly what he feels like saying or doing at the moment, with no true consideration of anyone else. The language each addresses to the one he momentarily thinks he loves is endlessly extravagant and ornamental, but it seems truly addressed to a relatively impersonal object of the speaker's romantic impulses. Lysander's last words before his eyes are anointed by Puck are vows of eternal love to Hermia; he is equally passionate to Helena a few lines later when he awakes to see her. When Hermia finally discovers him in the woods, she asks, 'But why unkindly didst thou leave me so?' Lysander's reply is both finely characteristic of his state and very funny: 'Why should he stay whom love doth press to go?' (III. ii. 184). A few lines later he is even more explicit, using the same rhyme: 'The hate I bare thee made me leave thee so' (190).

Victims of love-in-idleness frequently engage in chases (the pursuits and flights are often patterned as circles or mazes), confused verbal conflicts, attempts at physical combat, and reversals of traditional or genteel conventions of speech and action:

> Apollo flies, and Daphne holds the chase;
> The dove pursues the griffin, the mild hind
> Makes speed to catch the tiger . . .
>   (III. i. 231-3)

At one point Hermia chases Lysander, who chases Helena, who chases Demetrius, who had formerly chased Hermia and will soon chase Helena. For a number of lines Hermia tries to hold on to Lysander, primarily to keep him from fighting with Demetrius;[15] but when she finally thinks she understands that Helena has stolen Lysander's love ('You juggler! You canker-blossom!'—282), Hermia threatens to become the physical aggressor ('How low am I? I am not yet so low / But that my nails can reach unto thine eyes'—297-8), and Helena takes advantage of her new roles as favourite and potential victim as she pleads for masculine protection.[16] The scene is neatly reversed as Lysander and Demetrius compete in their efforts to restrain physically the raging Hermia:

Lysander. Be not afraid; she shall not harm thee, Helena.
Demetrius. No, sir, she shall not, though you take her part.   (321-2)

Harold Brooks remarked that in 'modern English' Hermia clamours 'to be "let get at" her tormentor';[17] the American for 'Let me come to her' (l. 328) would be simply 'Let me at her!'

As Lysander and Demetrius rush off-stage to fight, Helena flees from the angry Hermia; and Hermia follows the crowd—not knowing precisely why: 'I am amaz'd, and know not what to say' (344). But the darkness and Puck's ventriloquist challenges and mockeries frustrate the young men's attempts to engage in mortal combat as thoroughly as the earlier events of the night had prevented them from embracing their loves. Singly the men fall, exhausted and asleep, quite near to each other, vowing vengeance with daylight; and singly the women col-

---

15   *Lysander.* Away, you Ethiope!
        Demetrius.   No, no; he'll
        Seem to break loose—[*To Lysander*] take on as you would follow,
        But yet come not! You are a tame man, go!
        Lysander. Hang off, thou cat, thou burr! Vile thing, let loose,
        Or I will shake thee from me like a serpent.   (III. ii. 257-61)

        Demetrius. I wish I had your bond, for I perceive
        A weak bond holds you . . .   (267-8)

16   I pray you, though you mock me, gentlemen,
                    Let her not hurt me. I was never curst;
                    I have no gift for shrewishness;
                    I am a right maid for my cowardice;
                    Let her not strike me. You perhaps may think,
                    Because she is something lower than myself,
                    That I can match her.   (299-305)

17 Arden edition, p. cxiii.

lapse, close to the unseen men, Helena praying for light and a return to the ordinary world.[18] Hermia, who lasts longest of all and whose entrance is poignantly funny after Puck's 'Here she comes, curst and sad: / Cupid is a knavish lad / Thus to make poor females mad!' (439-41), prays for Lysander's safety, however intolerable his behaviour:

> Never so weary, never so in woe,
> Bedabbled with the dew, and torn with briars,
> I can no further crawl, no further go;
> My legs can keep no pace with my desires.
> Here will I rest me till the break of day. [*Lies down.*]
> Heavens shield Lysander, if they mean a fray! [*Sleeps*]
> (III. ii. 442-6)

Puck applies the remedy, Dian's bud, to Lysander's eyes, so that upon waking he will take 'True delight / In the sight / Of thy former lady's eye'. As Puck promises, the Jacks and Jills, as they awake, are properly paired off.

What are the differences between the wild confusions and shifts of the night of love-in-idleness and the stable true love that both comic convention and Oberon's later blessing ('So shall all the couples three / Ever true in loving be'—V. i. 393-4) assure us the lovers will finally achieve? The lovers have no clear idea of what has happened—or how, and of course Shakespeare was never so foolish as to attempt precise definitions of evanescent states, or formulaic solutions to impossible problems. But we can make a number of distinctions on the basis of what we see and hear within the course of the play. True love is not merely sexual attraction or appetite, although it is certainly associated with it. It cannot mean that reason has suddenly triumphed over everything else or that every successful lover has at last achieved the full self-knowledge of the ideal philosopher:[19] the lovers admit their ignorance along with their delight. It cannot be that they have finally conquered a magic enchantment that impinges on their inalienable, individual

----

[18]   Shine comforts, from the east
        That I may back to Athens by daylight,
        From these that my poor company detest.   (432-4)
[19] R. W. Dent anticipated this, as well as a number of my other points, in his splendid essay, 'Imagination in *A Midsummer Night's Dream*', *Shakespeare: 400* ed. J. G. McManaway (New York, 1964), pp. 115-29.

freedom: Demetrius never receives the remedy from Puck and will supposedly go through life happily enchanted by the magic eye-drops—although their effects on him have certainly changed by the end of the play. Puck's enchantment, moreover, hardly differs significantly from the earlier sorts of enchantment that the lovers were perfectly capable of succumbing to without any supernatural aids.

The differences between true and false love, active and idle love, seem more the results of differing actions and commitments than of differing sources or derivations or even immediate emotions. 'Love-in-idleness' may even be transformed into true love if it is, or becomes, reciprocal and if it can flourish in daylight and in an acknowledged relationship with a larger social world. No more than Lysander does Demetrius remember the details of what happened to him and to his emotions during the night; but he recognizes the powerful change that has taken place within him as the achievement or recovery of health, maturity, and natural joy, and he commits himself firmly to it as to something that will last his life:

> But my good lord, I wot not by what power—
> But by some power it is—my love to Hermia,
> Melted as the snow, seems to me now
> As the remembrance of an idle gaud
> Which in my childhood I did dote upon;
> And all the faith, the virtue of my heart,
> The object and the pleasure of mine eye,
> Is only Helena. To her, my lord,
> Was I betroth'd ere I saw Hermia;
> But like a sickness did I loathe this food:
> But as in health, come to my natural taste,
> Now I do wish it, love it, long for it,
> And will for evermore be true to it.   (IV. i. 163-74)

Demetrius sounds a bit like the Romeo who can hardly remember his infatuation with Rosaline. He feels he has awakened from a deluding dream.

When Theseus overrules Egeus (there can be no question of an enforced marriage after Demetrius has rejected Hermia) and announces plans for the triple wedding, the stunned lovers are left alone on stage, uncertain whether they dreamed or are still dreaming:

> *Demetrius.* These things seem small and undistinguishable,
>   Like far-off mountains turned into clouds.
> *Hermia.* Methinks I see these things with parted eye,
>   When everything seems double.   (IV. i. 186-9)

Helena, who has most reason to doubt the happy resolution of
her love, expresses her sudden discovery in a way that seems to
apply to all of them:

> And I have found Demetrius like a jewel,
>   Mine own, and not mine own.   (190-1)

Lovers do and do not 'belong to' each other. True lovers seem
to recognize and affirm the life of the other as existing apart
from the perceiving self, and delight that the loved one should
be other, as well as be miraculously capable of returning a
similar affirmation and affection. Beyond dreams of possession
of body and soul, as Milton's Samson remarked, 'love seeks to
have love'.[20] That search is essential to the 'intelligible flame
not in Paradise to be resisted'.[21] And once firmly fixed, love
seeks primarily the good of the other. In an extreme situation,
one far from the thoughts or experience of these lovers joyfully
approaching marriage, a lover might truly be willing to die in
order that his loved one might live.

It is Demetrius who formulates the ultimate questions for the
lovers on stage and for the audience:

>   Are you sure
>   That we are awake? It seems to me
>   That yet we sleep, we dream.   (191-3)

His method for attempting to distinguish between dream and
reality, sleeping and waking, however unconvincing in terms
of logic or metaphysics, is fully convincing for the lovers and
for most of our unphilosophical daily lives:

>   Do not you think
>   The Duke was here, and bid us follow him?
> *Hermia.* Yea, and my father.
> *Helena.*   And Hippolyta.

---

[20] *Samson Agonistes*, l. 837.
[21] *The Doctrine and Discipline of Divorce*, Book I, ch. iv; *John Milton: Complete Poems and Major Prose*, ed. Merritt Y. Hughes (New York, 1957), p. 709.

Lysander. And he did bid us follow to the temple.
Demetrius. Why then, we are awake: let's follow him,
 And by the way let us recount our dreams.   (193-8)

If we dream the same dream, we believe that we are awake. Perhaps that is as near as the human imagination can come to determining reality. The recurrent dreams of both comedies and weddings (like those of tragedies and funerals) suggest that the collective dreams usually rule both on and off stage.

Theseus, with his refusal to believe the lovers' stories (and since the lovers never know of the fairies' interventions, those stories must have been a good deal less fantastic than what we have seen and heard on-stage) and with his grouping together of lunatics, lovers, and poets as madly unreliable, was sometimes in the past accepted as the mature voice of reason and reality; today, when reason is frequently considered less reliable than either emotion or the imagination, he is sometimes dismissed as a hopeless philistine—despite his poetry. At any rate, Hippolyta has the last word on the subject, and she reinforces the lovers' acceptance of both the strangeness and the power of minds that are transformed together in love:

> But all the story of the night told over,
> And all their minds transfigur'd so together,
> More witnesseth than fancy's images,
> And grows to something of great constancy;
> But howsoever, strange and admirable.
>   (V. i. 23-7)[22]

After the wonderfully farcical production and reception of 'Pyramus and Thisbe', the lovers are off to bed, and the fairies return to bless the house and the beds. Puck's epilogue to the audience seems doubly disingenuous:

> If we shadows have offended,
> Think but this, and all is mended,
> That you have but slumber'd here

[22] L. A. Beaurline has suggested that we do not have to choose between those two: 'Dramatic action has so interplayed with unnatural perspectives that the known and the strange unknown became entangled. Theseus is making a good joke that betrays his foolish wisdom, and in a glimmer of thought, his wise folly; so Shakespeare makes a self-deprecating joke about his play, also very much in character. . . . Both Theseus and Hippolyta are aware of part of the mystery, but in the eyes of the audience the two views are as married as their spokesman [*sic*].' *Jonson and Elizabethan Comedy: Essays in Dramatic Rhetoric* (San Marino, 1978), pp. 101-2.

> While these visions did appear.
> And this weak and idle theme,
> No more yielding but a dream,
> Gentles, do not reprehend:
> If you pardon, we will mend.   (V. i. 409-16)

Despite Pepys, there can rarely have been occasions when the play, if at all decently performed, has failed to delight a substantial part of its audience; and it has clearly demonstrated that the dream, rather than a 'weak and idle theme', is something strange, admirable, and of great constancy.

Although dreams of love must be related to the realities of power if the love is ever to proceed from idleness to action, on their wedding night the confident lovers are not much concerned with questions of power. There have, of course, been many instances of threatening powers before: Egeus melodramatically asserting a father's authority and calling for either his daughter's obedience or her death; Theseus and the authority of the law; Theseus and Hippolyta and the war between the Athenians and the Amazons; the war of the elements unleashed by a discordant transcendental marriage; physical pursuits and attempted flights and duels; the power of love-in-idleness concentrated so that it can be administered by Oberon and Puck; threats of rape or other violence. But from the time the lovers awake together and Theseus overrules Egeus, these no longer threaten: the relaxed and playful assurance of the lovers as they watch the attempted portrayal of the flight of Pyramus and Thisbe from parental authority to the woods, the threat of the lion, and, in the event, the hilarious double suicide, make that clear. When order has been re-established sufficiently to give assurance that the human enterprise will continue in a manner not immediately threatening to lovers, neither the lovers nor the audience of comedy are much concerned with matters of authority: no one now flees his proper love. But as we are invited to share the dream, we are also nudged to recognize it *as* a dream, a vision of delight limited by age and time and occasion that we can rarely possess fully or for long without a 'translation' more profound and more enduring than Bottom's. The *literary* miracle of *A Midsummer Night's Dream* is that the magic of its momentary dream is repeatable on any occasion when we are capable of responding imaginatively to youth and to intelligent reading of the lines.

Perhaps older observers, like some self-consciously serious younger members of theatrical audiences, are ordinarily more concerned with dreams of power. Such dreams may range from those of supreme personal power over a world or even a universe (as with Tamburlane and Milton's Satan) to less megalomaniacal and seemingly more realizable dreams of power within a section of the world, a nation, a social or political group, a family, or a personal relationship. As the dreams move from fantasy to action, they may be temporarily or partly achieved; but they are threatened, never absolute, within this waking life of time, change, and mortality. This is largely the realm of Shakespeare's histories, his tragedies, and to some degree of his tragicomedies or romances. Only occasionally can the dreams of power be regarded as simply or unmitigatedly evil or unnatural. Social and political order, necessary for the welfare of human beings, necessarily implies power; and however ideal or collective its form, some individuals must assume power and use it. The history plays explore recurrent problems: since either the extreme abuse or the total neglect of power will probably, if not inevitably, be ended by usurpation, revolt or death, how can a new power be established that seems legitimate, or achieves legitimacy? And how can the inevitable successions of power, from individual to individual and generation to generation, be achieved with least loss and destruction to the state or the society? The tragedies usually filter such questions through a primary concern with the defeat, destruction, and death of a heroic figure or heroic figures.

It is within the late romances that the themes of power and love are most hauntingly related both to each other and to dreams. Fitzroy Pyle remarked that *The Winter's Tale* was 'in some ways' 'a companion piece' to *A Midsummer Night's Dream* ('both plays have their eye on the *Metamorphoses*')[23] and some nineteenth-century commentators thought the two plays resembled each other in their errors and incompetence.[24] But

23 *The Winter's Tale: A Commentary on the Structure* (London, 1969), p. 2.
24 In his New Variorum edition of *The Winter's Tale* (Philadelphia, 1898), p. 6, Horace H. Furness cited several relevant instances. W. W. Lloyd remarked in S. W. Singer's second edition (1856), p. 133, 'The title suggests that it is in some manner a pendant of *The Midsummer Night's Dream*. The classic and romantic, the pagan and

The Winter's Tale explores fully the abuses and even horrors of power, the possibilities of destruction and death, which are suppressed or deflected from our central concerns within *A Midsummer Night's Dream*; its final vision of a happy ending with the triumph of love and of time is more literally fabulous and more moving than the wonderful comic ending of the earlier play.

chivalric, are huddled and combined here as there, and still more glaringly and unscrupulously.' In his first edition of 1872, p. 272, R. G. White stated, 'Shakespeare sought only to put a very popular story into dramatic form; and of this he advertised his hearers by calling this play a Tale, just as before he called a play similarly wanting in dramatic interest a Dream.'

II

Dreams of Love and Power:
The Winter's Tale

Beginning with the second scene of *The Winter's Tale*, we watch Leontes as, misinterpreting his wife's actions and gestures and language, he is possessed by a nightmarish jealousy which destroys his love and leads him to attempt to destroy everything and everyone closest to him: his friend, his wife, his daughter. By the mid-point of the play he has actually caused the deaths of his son and his faithful servant Antigonus, he believes he has killed his wife and his daughter, and he looks forward to a lifetime of sorrow and penance: his story seems indeed one of endless winter. His situation has been in some ways more horrifying than Othello's, for he has managed to deceive himself and destroy his happiness without the help of an Iago; he is the victim of no one but himself. But rather than being invited to analyse and judge his moral flaws (as if we shared the duties and authority of casuists or confessional priests) or even to devote our chief energies to determining exactly why the nightmare occurred (as if we were primarily psychologists or moral historians), we spectators are led by the opening scenes, I believe, to empathy and a shocked sense of possible identification with Leontes' madness—to the conviction that it, or something like it, could happen to us, and that it would mean, horribly, our destruction. We are almost overcome by the vision of a delusion which, with no conscious moment of a devil's bargain, blossoms to paranoia and madness before our eyes and ears to the point where, quite literally, 'nothing is, but what is not':[1]

> Is whispering nothing?
> Is leaning cheek to cheek? is meeting noses?
> Kissing with inside lip? stopping the career

---

[1] *Macbeth*, I. iii. 142. I quote *The Winter's Tale* throughout from the text of J. H. P. Pafford's Arden edition (London, 1963). I owe a number of my perceptions about the play to Joan Hartwig's *Shakespeare's Tragicomic Vision* (Baton Rouge, 1972).

Of laughter with a sigh (a note infallible
Of breaking honesty)? horsing foot on foot?
Skulking in corners? wishing clocks more swift?
Hours, minutes? noon, midnight? and all eyes
Blind with the pin and web, but theirs; theirs only.
That would unseen be wicked? is this nothing?
Why then the world, and all that's in't, is nothing,
The covering sky is nothing, Bohemia nothing,
My wife is nothing, nor nothing have these nothings,
If this be nothing.   (I. ii. 284-96)

In their hysteria and sexual nausea, Leontes' 'imaginations' are indeed 'as foul / As Vulcan's stithy'.[2] And that we might be moved to share them is threatened openly in one of the most uncomfortable speeches in Shakespeare's plays, when Leontes directly addresses the theatrical audience:

                                    There have been,
(Or I am much deceiv'd) cuckolds ere now,
And many a man there is (even at this present,
Now, while I speak this) holds his wife by th' arm,
That little thinks she has been sluic'd in 's absence
And his pond fish'd by his next neighbour, by
Sir Smile, his neighbour: nay, there's comfort in't,
Whiles other men have gates, and those gates open'd,
As mine, against their will.   (I. ii. 190-8)

It is a fortunate man who, feeling comfortably superior to that insistent present tense and, later, the sinister modulation to the first-person plural in 'many thousands on 's / Have the disease, and feel 't not', (206-7) can unselfconsciously keep his arm linked to his wife's in the theatre.

We may also feel threatened that Leontes' obsession should arise so suddenly from such casual circumstances. But before we met Leontes, we saw in the brief opening scene between Camillo and Archidamus[3] how the language of courtesy can be

---

[2] *Hamlet*, III. ii. 83-4.

[3] There seems little agreement among the critics concerning either the tone or the purpose of the scene. In *The Winter's Tale: A Study* (London, 1947), p. 41, S. L. Bethell seemed to suggest that the speeches here intentionally burlesqued court style, while J. H. P. Pafford considered the 'opening conversational prose . . . a kindly, courtly language' (Arden edition, p. lxxxiv). Howard Felperin thinks the style of the opening scene 'perfectly colloquial' ('Given the Courtly setting'), but seems to think its 'oracular' nature most significantly anticipates the 'romantic nature of the play and its miraculous happy ending' (*Shakespearean Romance*, Princeton, 1972, p. 223). In his fine,

exaggerated and misinterpreted so that it may, if not questioned or opposed, create discomfort and misunderstanding. When we hear the opening lines in the theatre, I believe that we are most obviously first struck by the way in which the language of those unknown speakers, engaged initially in courtly compliment and protest and then in courtly description of a royal friendship and the promise of the young prince Mamillius, becomes extravagantly in excess of what seems proper for the occasion or matter described, until each of the speakers in turn is interrupted and his extravagance gently rebuked:

Camillo. I think, this coming summer, the King of Sicilia means to pay Bohemia the visitation which he justly owes him.
Archidamus. Wherein our entertainment shall shame us, we will be justified in our loves: for indeed—
Camillo. Beseech you—
Archidamus. Verily I speak it in the freedom of my knowledge: we cannot with such magnificent—in so rare—I know not what to say—We will give you sleepy drinks, that your senses (unintelligent of our insufficience) may, though they cannot praise us, as little accuse us.
Camillo. You pay a great deal too dear for what's given freely.

(I. i. 5-18)[4]

Archidamus. You have an unspeakable comfort of your young prince Mamillius: it is a gentleman of the greatest promise that ever came into my note.
Camillo. I very well agree with you in the hopes of him: it is a gallant child; one that, indeed, physics the subject, makes old hearts fresh: they that went on crutches ere he was born desire yet their life to see him a man.
Archidamus. Would they else be content to die?
Camillo. Yes; if there were no other excuse why they should desire to live.

comprehensive study, Charles Frey assumes the simple 'sincerity' of both speakers, and thinks that Archidamus represents bucolic virtues and in his central speech 'proceeds to enact a kind of hesitant groping down from the surface of courtly compliment to the fount of integrity and clear will. . . . Shakespeare shows minds groping past flawed performances, magnificent and impersonal entertainment, persons and actions maimed and on crutches, toward the truest and freshest sources of social harmony—justifying love, honesty, the comfort of youth' (*Shakespeare's Vast Romance: A Study of 'The Winter's Tale'*, Columbia and London, 1980, pp. 55-6).

4 I follow Charles Frey in reading a comma, instead of the colon of the Folio and the Arden edition, after 'shame us' in line 8.

Archidamus. If the king had no son, they would desire to live on crutches till he had one. (I. i. 34-45)

Archidamus's exit line nearly always causes laughter in the
theatre: however wonderful the child, most aged observers
would want to continue living even without him. Earlier, too,
there may have been some smiles if not open laughter at the extravagance of Archidamus's protests: fulsomely grateful guests
who insist on their inability to reciprocate hospitality can prove
embarrassing or even offensive. Hyperbolical language often
raises questions of tone. While it may invite scepticism concerning the speaker's sincerity or even comic deflation, it may also,
as we soon discover, give rise to fatal misinterpretation. Yet
such language is inevitably used (and frequently approaches
incoherence), not only in the ordinary exchanges of courtesy
and love but also whenever any speaker believes (or wishes
others to believe) that he has glimpsed a reality or an appearance literally beyond words. In the same scene when Camillo
explains that Sicily's hospitality has not been excessive because
of the length and intensity of the two kings' mutual affection,
Archidamus responds, 'I think there is not in the world either
malice or matter to alter it' (11. 33-4). He is right: the alter-
ation begins with Leontes' ignorance rather than his malice,
and there is no 'matter' but Leontes' disastrous misreading of
the language and gestures of courtesy and proper love.

I am not entirely convinced by the argument that in the second
scene the audience not only shares but also anticipates Leontes'
suspicion of the relations between Hermione and Polixenes,
but William Matchett clearly demonstrates the tissue of possible sexual suggestions or innuendoes, throughout the scene;[5]
certainly we can understand and respond to the ways Leontes
interprets them, and we may actually wince at the dreadful
way in which they accumulate into an increasingly sinister mass
of circumstantial evidence. Hermione's pregnant figure and
Polixenes' reference to the nine months of his visit; the uses of
'burden' and the 'cipher' that can 'multiply'; Hermione's expressed willingness to allow Leontes to stay longer in Bohemia
than Polixenes has stayed in Sicily; phrases such as 'limber

---

[5] 'Some Dramatic Techniques in *The Winter's Tale*', *Shakespeare Survey 22* (1969), pp.
93-107.

vows', 'a lady's Verily's / As potent as a lord's' (I. ii. 50-1), 'kind hostess', and particularly Hermione's remark to Polix- enes, 'Th' offences we have made you do, we'll answer, / If you first sinn'd with us, and that with us / You did continue fault, and that you slipp'd not / With any but with us' (83-6) —in which 'you', 'we', and 'us' become horribly ambiguous; Polixenes' capitulation to Hermione after he had refused Leon- tes; Hermione's responses to Leontes, 'You may ride's / With one soft kiss a thousand furlongs ere / With spur we heat an acre' (94-6), and 'I have spoke to th' purpose twice: / The one, for ever earn'd a royal husband; / Th' other, for some while a friend' (106-8): these, even without the repeated smiles and the clasped hands, are enough to cause Leontes' *tremor cordis*. And after his initial seizure, suggestive phrases continue to reinforce his obsession: 'You look / As if you held a brow of much distraction' from Hermione just as Leontes has felt his horns growing; Leontes' obsession with 'play'; Camillo's 'At the good queen's entreaty' (220) and 'To satisfy your highness, and the entreaties / Of our most gracious mistress' (232-3). Everything here derives from one of the most ordinary social gestures: the host's and hostess's insistence, 'Oh, you must stay longer!' But Leontes leaps to the conviction of his betrayal: his faith in his wife is destroyed.

Charles Frey has described succinctly the horrifying pattern of the subsequent action:

Leontes appears four times and each time does the same thing: he denounces Hermione or her surrogate, Paulina, and is rebuked by representatives of the court. To be more precise, in a theme with little variation, Leontes four times expresses his misogyny, separates mother from child, and confronts indignant bystanders. . . . As the audience *hears* Leontes conceive his jealousy, accuse Hermione, debate Paulina, and conduct the trial, it also *sees* him rejecting advice and comfort, dismissing women, losing company, being left alone, so that, while he orally projects an image of alienated man, he icono- graphically enacts the part as well.[6]

Suddenly become a mad structuralist who reads all the signs in one destructive fashion, Leontes provides a wrenching image of how paranoia may create something like the social situations it

---

[6] *Shakespeare's Vast Romance*, pp. 127-8.

has first imagined. By the end of Act III, scene ii, if not before, an attentive viewer may feel like echoing the questions of Sonia to Raskolnikov in *Crime and Punishment*: 'What have you done! —what have you done to yourself!'[7]

At the same time, however, we become increasingly concerned with the victims of Leontes in these opening scenes. Our sense of possible identification with his delusions, crimes, and isolation is deflected by his status and his manner as a monarch: he claims to possess a power more nearly absolute than anything most of us can imagine or desire:

> What, what need we
> Commune with you of this, but rather follow
> Our forceful instigation? Our prerogative
> Calls not your counsels, but our natural goodness
> Imparts this; which if you, or stupefied,
> Or seeming so, in skill, cannot or will not
> Relish a truth like us, inform yourselves
> We need no more of your advice . . .   (II. i. 161-8)[8]

He sends to the oracle only to 'Give rest to th' minds of others'; he is utterly satisfied with what he 'knows' (II. i. 189-91).

We are comforted in the first half of the play by another pattern of action that includes almost everyone else and that opposes the pattern which Leontes has established. Frey describes it:

What the audience sees when Leontes is onstage is opposition leading to static isolation. What it sees when he is offstage is cooperation leading to the forward movement of a pair. . . . [Archidamus and Camillo] pass across the stage in final amity. After Leontes reveals his jealousy, Camillo meets Polixenes and they decide to escape together. We see them pass across the stage as friends. Paulina, in the prison, gathers Emilia to her purpose and exits with her. Cleomenes and Dion marvel at their Delphic journey and hasten forward to court.[9]

---

[7] Fyodor Dostoevsky, *Crime and Punishment*, trans. Constance Garnett (New York, 1919), p. 371. At the opening of the final act, Leontes comes to a recognition analogous to Sonia's: 'Whilst I remember / Her, and her virtues, I cannot forget / My blemishes in them, and so still think of / The wrong I did myself' (V. i. 6-9).

[8] I follow G. Blakemore Evans's text (*The Riverside Shakespeare*, Boston, 1974) in omitting the comma of the Folio and the Arden edition after 'truth' in line 167.

[9] *Shakespeare's Vast Romance*, pp. 132-3. David Richman has perceptively remarked that a major difference between Leontes and a Macbeth or Othello or even a Richard III is that Leontes lacks willing instruments to carry out his intents.

The violence of Leontes unites the others into an opposing community of sanity and charity.

It may also be of comfort to us that this man who claims such absolute power is continually faced with the actual limitations of his power. He cannot plan for full vengeance because Polixenes is 'in himself too mighty, / And in his parties, his alliance' (II. iii. 20-1). Leontes imagines that his courtiers know of, and gossip about, his disgrace (I. ii. 222-8) and that Camillo and Polixenes are laughing at him (II. iii. 23-4), but he is powerless to silence the former or to punish the latter. He cannot control either the opinions or the actions of those around him: 'What! lack I credit?' (II. i. 157). He cannot determine the effects of royal or judicial ceremonies, the judgement of Apollo, or the issues of life and death.[10] We are unlikely to anticipate an absolutely unhappy ending for a play when the power of evil is so clearly limited, when the evil itself seems to be a matter of individual delusion rather than of individual or general conspiracy or corruption, and when nature, men, and women unite to protect the innocent.

Hermione, the most clearly noble character, demonstrates how the community may oppose Leontes' delusion, tyranny, and scurrility without becoming contaminated by them or sinking to his level of discourse. Hermione neither falters nor lapses into shrillness:

> How will this grieve you,
> When you shall come to clearer knowledge, that
> You thus have publish'd me! Gentle my lord,
> You scarce can right me throughly, then, to say
> You did mistake. (II. i. 96-100)

[10] In soliloquy (I. ii. 357-61) Camillo states extravagantly that he would not poison Polixenes even if he could find example 'Of thousands that had struck anointed kings / And flourish'd after'; 'but since / Nor brass nor stone, nor parchment bears not one, / Let villainy itself forswear't'. This has sometimes been read as a particular instance of Shakespeare's flattery of Stuart notions of absolutism and the divine right of kings. But if he paid close attention to the context, James I could have taken only questionable pleasure in an argument that because of the sanctity of *any* anointed king, a courtier ordered to kill one must disobey his own monarch, flee, and undertake a new allegiance: the complex political and moral implications are hardly consoling to simple-minded notions of absolute sovereignty. At the end of Act III, scene ii, the repentant Leontes praises Camillo as 'a man of truth, of mercy' (I. 157), 'most humane / And fill'd with honour' (ll. 165-6) in that he had resisted Leontes' own threats and promises of rewards and had betrayed the planned assassination of Polixenes. By this point Leontes has come to perceive his own jealousy and murderous plot as an unnatural aberration or seizure, and Camillo's actions as loyalty to his true self.

> Adieu, my lord:
> I never wish'd to see you sorry; now
> I trust I shall.   (II. i. 122-4)

It is she who possesses real and unquestioned power. When Leontes orders 'Away with her, to prison!' (II. i. 103) none of his attendants moves to obey—not even after his later 'Shall I be heard?'. It is only after Hermione's 'Adieu, my lord' (1. 122) and *her* order ('My women, come; you have leave'— l.124) that the queen, the ladies, and supposedly the attendants or guards move to depart. In context, Leontes' accompanying 'Go, do our bidding: hence!' (1. 125) seems weakly petulant. In the judgement scene, Hermione, completely unafraid and almost welcoming death, still firmly asserts her honour, denounces injustice, and appeals to the oracle of Apollo.

It is important for the response of the audience that the threats to, and ironical defeats of, Leontes' claims to power are often associated either with open laughter that undermines their seriousness or with a sense of the miraculous, supernatural judgement, or providential wonder;[11] both the laughter and the wonder anticipate the contrasting movements and values of the second half of the play. At the turning-point, immediately after Antigonus is chased off-stage by the bear, when the Shepherd discovers the infant Perdita and then is joined by the Clown, the providentially miraculous and the laughter are joined.

Most of the early laughter is associated with Paulina, the choral, fearless truth-teller who denounces abused authority and madness. Like the Fool in *King Lear*, she becomes the comic centre of the first part of the play—a position that Autolycus takes in the second half. The distance between the broadness of the laughter she frequently evokes and the uneasiness with which an audience often responds to the 'bitter Fool' is related not only to the fact that *The Winter's Tale* is a romance

---

[11] The miraculous and providential are most notably evoked in the brief scene (III. i) in which the astonished Cleomenes and Dion recall the glorious wonders of 'Delphos' and the oracle of Apollo; but something of the providential is suggested also by the friendship and escape of Camillo and Polixenes, the unity of the courtiers in support of Hermione, and Hermione's appeal to the oracle; and Leontes interprets the death of Mamillius as evidence of Apollo's anger and punishment: 'Apollo's angry, and the heavens themselves / Do strike at my injustice' (III. ii. 146-7).

and *King Lear* a tragedy, but also to Paulina's descent from a
long line of comic stage shrews who reduce to absurdity
masculine claims to superior authority.[12] Paulina, however, is
not simply a wilful shrew, but the good shrew who happily takes
on the duty of stating truth:

> These dangerous, unsafe lunes i' th' king, beshrew them!
> He must be told on't, and he shall: the office
> Becomes a woman best. I'll take't upon me:
> If I prove honey-mouth'd, let my tongue blister,
> And never to my red-look'd anger be
> The trumpet any more.   (II. ii. 30-5)

While Leontes perceives or manufactures endless ambiguities
of tone or moral implication within language, Paulina insistently hammers out the ironic possibilities:

>   I say, I come
> From your good queen.
> *Leontes.*   Good queen!
> *Paulina.* Good queen, my lord, good queen: I say good queen,
>   And would by combat make her good, so were I
>   A man, the worst about you.
> *Leontes.*   Force her hence.
> *Paulina.* Let him that makes but trifles of his eyes
>   First hand me: on mine own accord I'll off;
>   But first, I'll do my errand. The good queen
>   (For she is good) hath brought you forth a daughter;
>   Here 'tis; [*laying down the child*] commends it to your blessing.
>   (II. iii. 57-66)

From the moment that she enters with the infant Perdita in her
arms, Paulina is wonderfully assured. She charges that the pusil-
lanimity of the ceremonious masculine courtiers feeds the king's
dangerous madness. When Leontes recognizes that she has
dared to enter his presence, he exclaims, 'How! / Away with
that audacious lady! Antigonus, / I charg'd thee that she
should not come about me. / I knew she would' (II. iii. 41-4).
That petulant last phrase almost inevitably causes laughter in
the theatre. Similar laughing punctuates the scene until Paulina's exit:

---

12 At a conference on *The Winter's Tale* at the University of Rochester in the spring
of 1978, Elizabeth Kinkaid-Ehlers read a paper that defined persuasively Paulina's
role and its relationship to the roles of Hermione and Perdita.

> *Leontes.*   Traitors!
> Will you not push her out? Give her the bastard,
> Thou dotard! thou art woman-tir'd, unroosted
> By thy dame Partlet here. Take up the bastard,
> Take 't up, I say; give 't to thy crone.
> *Paulina.*   For ever
> Unvenerable be thy hands, if thou
> Tak'st up the princess, by that forced baseness
> Which he has put upon 't!
> *Leontes.*   He dreads his wife.
> *Paulina.* So I would you did; then 'twere past all doubt
> You'd call your children yours.   (II. iii. 72-81)

> *Leontes.*   A gross hag!
> And, lozel, thou art worthy to be hang'd,
> That wilt not stay her tongue.
> *Antigonus.*   Hang all the husbands
> That cannot do that feat, you'll leave yourself
> Hardly one subject.   (107-11)

There is no limit to the violence of Leontes' language; but we
laugh because the violence has none of its intended effects: no
one moves to obey Leontes' orders, and Paulina comically
desacralizes the fatal language of royal power and civil judgement by refusing to take it seriously.[13] When his courtiers finally move to obey one of Leontes' relatively harmless commands (if they cannot shut up this irreverent woman, they
should at least get her out of his sight), Paulina easily resists
them, reproves them, and leaves on her own dignified terms:

> *Leontes.*   On your allegiance,
> Out of the chamber with her! Were I a tyrant,
> Where were her life? she durst not call me so,
> If she did know me one. Away with her!
> *Paulina.* I pray you, do not push me; I'll be gone.
> Look to your babe, my lord: 'tis yours: Jove send her
> A better guiding spirit! What needs these hands?
> You, that are thus so tender o'er his follies,
> Will never do him good, not one of you.
> So, so: farewell; we are gone.   (120-9)

---

[13] In this single respect Paulina's role is comparable to Barnardine's in *Measure for Measure*, IV. iii, when he refuses to prepare for death because he insists on sleeping off his hangover.

It is difficult to imagine that an audience responding to these lines could seriously anticipate that this play will be a tragedy. Paulina will continue equally fearless and outspoken, if much less comic, when she devotes her energies to denouncing Leontes for murderous stupidity and, through fifteen or sixteen years, to keeping him up to his formal penance. At this point, however, in a society in which the moral order is turned upside-down and authoritative heretics plan to burn the true believers but have not yet taken any lives, comic subversion and promise can firmly embody truth, faith, loyalty, and normal family relationships. Later, in a world of repentant rulers and young lovers, where the lost may be recovered and new life promised, comic subversion, largely in the form of Autolycus, can afford to be thoroughly amoral, devoted to deception as well as play, with only its most injurious efforts for personal aggrandizement somewhat curtailed or deflected by overwhelmingly providential developments.

Before Time personally intervenes, the second part of the play has already begun at the moment when the Shepherd enters, complaining of the sexual and general disorderliness and irresponsibility of the young:

I would there were no age between ten and three-and-twenty, or that youth would sleep out the rest; for there is nothing in the between but getting wenches with child, wronging the ancientry, stealing, fighting.

(III. iii. 59-63)

The old shepherd considers human nature—at least in youth— as generally corrupt as Leontes does; but rather than being horrified or haunted by it, he finds it merely an annoying inconvenience, exemplified by those obstreperous young hunters who have frightened away two of his best sheep. When he finds the baby, he is delighted ('A very pretty barne! . . . A pretty one; a very pretty one'—ll. 70-1), assumes it is a courtly by-blow, and immediately plans to 'take it up for pity' (l. 76)—and evidently for pleasure, too.

When the Clown, his son, joins him, excited to incoherence by the horrors he has witnessed on both land and water, we are even more clearly in a comic, rural stage-world far removed from direct and serious concerns with matter of state or tragic emotions. What he has seen is as physically horrendous as any of Leontes' threatened acts of revenge, and almost as astonishing as any of the ballads which will so fascinate the Clown later. But his language distances us remarkably from what he tries to describe:

But to make an end of the ship, to see how the sea flap-dragoned it: but first, how the poor souls roared, and the sea mocked them: and how the poor gentleman roared, and the bear mocked him, both roaring louder than the sea or weather. . . . I have not winked since I saw these sights: the men are not yet cold under water, nor the bear half dined on the gentleman: he's at it now.   (III. iii. 97-105)

The chief burden of the speech becomes neither the fates of Antigonus and the sailors nor the Clown's responses to them, but the comic inappropriateness of his language: 'flap-dragoned it', 'half dined on the gentleman'. Our laughter is increased by the suddenness of the play's shift in tone and perhaps also by our uneasy recognition that the Clown's excitement is only an extreme example of the familiar human proclivity to find reports of horrors or disasters shamefully titillating.

But both we and the two figures on stage quickly forget the horrors as they turn to the child:

But look thee here, boy. Now bless thyself: thou met'st with things dying, I with things new-born.   (111-13)

With the discovery of the gold the stage figures rejoice in the expectation of a changed and prosperous life. The Clown will return only for one 'good deed'—to bury Antigonus—'if there be any of him left' (129). ''Tis a lucky day, boy, and we'll do good deeds on 't' (136).

When Time intervenes to explain that he will 'give my scene such growing / As you had slept between' (IV. i. 16-17), he relates the dreams of the audience to the dreams of the characters on stage in a way that may remind us of Puck. But Time warns that he never pleases all and that, however percipient we imagine ourselves, we cannot absolutely predict the events of the future, here or elsewhere (cf. IV. i. 1-4). He reminds us that it is in his power 'To o'erthrow law, and in one self-born hour / To plant and o'erwhelm custom' (ll. 8-9). Despite those claims, if we know any romances at all, we *do* know at least part of what will happen from the moment that the infant

Perdita, ignored by the bear, is discovered by the Shepherd. But we do not know exactly how it will happen, and we certainly do not anticipate all that will happen: while we surely look forward to the happy recovery of the lost royal princess, the play will provide us with plenty of surprises. John Taylor has described the movement of the play after the appearance of the bear as 'spasmodic, some of its episodes apparently mere interludes, its tone shifting crazily'.[14] The scene with Polixenes and Camillo 'seems to put us back into the flow of the action, but when Autolycus enters singing it is as if out of nowhere'. By the time Florizel and Perdita enter, 'we have nearly surrendered up our sense of what rightly belongs' within the play:

The surrender, which is the beginning of our patience, is a result of a delight with the art before us more than the life it depicts; we respond to the whimsical play of Time's glass, more than what it actually measures or mirrors, for only with the appearance of Perdita in the next scene will life itself seem wonderful. The action has lost its greatness and urgency, and what seems to carry us along is a continuous amazement in theatrical variety and zest.[15]

The fact that no one in the second half of the play is as obsessively and despairingly concerned with power as Leontes was in the first half helps make dramatically possible those remarkable shifts in the method of the play and the responses of the audience. Polixenes, of course, is insistent on a proper royal marriage for a properly dutiful son, and he can momentarily fall into a violent anger—threatening to disown Florizel and torture or put to death Perdita and the Shepherd—that faintly echoes Leontes' murderous rage. Like Leontes', too, his outburst is based upon his interpretation of the language and attitude of his loved one. But in contrast to Leontes, Polixenes is incensed by a truly careless, if not callous, expression:[16] when the Shepherd promises to make Perdita's 'portion equal his', Florizel jauntily replies,

O, that must be
I' th' virtue of your daughter: one being dead,

14 'The Patience of *The Winter's Tale*', *Essays in Criticism*, 23 (1973), 349.
15 'The Patience of *The Winter's Tale*', 349-50.
16 Taylor (p. 332) is one of the few critics who comment on how shocking Florizel's lines are.

I shall have more than you can dream of yet;
Enough then for your wonder. But come on,
Contract us 'fore these witnesses.

(IV. iv. 387-91)

In Polixenes' presence, Florizel's gloating expectation of extra-ordinary riches with his father's death is as shocking and as embarrassing as it would have been had Theseus's mother been listening when he compared his longing for his wedding night to a young man's typical longing for a dowager's death. But however insensitively expressed, Florizel's emotion is more normal and more forgivable (as young people must, biologi-cally and biblically, abandon parents for wives and husbands) than the sort of betrayal Leontes imagined; and Polixenes acts out no part of his momentary fantasy of revenge. In the second half of the play the dreams are primarily of desire for love and delight rather than nightmares of betrayal, loss, and the desire for power and revenge; and almost all of them are fulfilled—including those of Polixenes for a loving and noble son and a noble daughter-in-law, and even Leontes' dream of things which go beyond what any human being truly expects in this world: the recovery of the lost and the dead.

The range of dreams for all the dreamers within the second half of *The Winter's Tale* goes far beyond the dreams within *A Midsummer Night's Dream*. Camillo dreams of returning to Sicilia and of reconciliation with Leontes. The Shepherd and the Clown dream of fairy gold, lucky lives, and a grand sheep-shearing festival; and after the brief (and, for the audience, comic) nightmare of royal displeasure and fears of torment and death, they dream of a 'preposterous estate' (V. ii. 147-8), each as 'a gentleman born'—'any time these four hours' (V. ii. 134-7)—with royal kindred. The Clown's parody of Auto-lycus's former parody of an arrogant courtier's behaviour towards the lower orders is rendered laughably harmless by the Shepherd's plea that 'we must be gentle, now we are gentle-men' (V. ii. 152-3) and by the Clown's assurance that he will swear like a gentleman to friendly lies.

Autolycus appears suddenly, as if spring, with its renewed energies and appetites, came immediately after the dead of winter. His song of ale, linen for the stealing, and romps in the hay with his 'aunts' seems almost incidental to his delight as an artist—a con artist. He takes more pleasure in the elaborate, reversed Good Samaritan dodge by which he picks the Clown's pocket than in the pocket's contents; and no matter how up-standing they may be outside the theatre, most members of the audience identify with this clever knave as he cozens fools:

Softly, dear sir [*Picks his pocket*]; good sir, softly. You ha' done me a charitable office.   (IV. iii. 75-6)

When the Clown starts to reach for his missing purse to offer Autolycus money, we laugh at Autolycus's protests at the same time that we hope he will get away with his theft:

No, good sweet sir; no, I beseech you, sir: I have a kinsman not past three-quarters of a mile hence, unto whom I was going: I shall there have money, or anything I want: offer me no money, I pray you; that kills my heart.   (IV. iii. 78-82)

Autolycus is not possessed by dreams; he manufactures and sells them, both in his singing commercials for all the love trinkets guaranteed to convey or arouse love and in those hor-rendous ballads that so charm his hearers that they are literally rapt—unconscious—when he 'gelds' a codpiece or 'pinches' a placket. He is so sure of his skill and his power that he fre-quently sings or speaks directly to his audience—off stage as well as on: if anyone loses a purse during the performance, he cannot claim that Autolycus failed to warn him. But he is no evil Circe who enchants in order to enslave or possess utterly her hearers; he seeks only a temporary advantage (he does no serious harm to anyone in the play), and he chiefly enjoys the game of enchantment itself. Still, his art is removed from (indeed, it is almost a parody of) the greater arts of Nature and miraculous providence which ultimately triumph in the play. Autolycus's songs and ballads present the meretricious (bugle bracelets and tawdry lace), the grotesque (unkind women transformed into singing fish), and the scandalously unnatural (wives of usurers who desire to eat adders' heads before they give birth to money-bags) as literal facts rather than as imagin-ative constructions; instead of awakening their hearers to both reality and wondrous possibilities, the songs and ballads lull them into unconsciousness, a 'time of lethargy' (IV. iv. 615) so deep that they recognize neither themselves (here they may resemble Bottom and his crew) nor the fact that they are being robbed. However remotely descended from Mercury, Autolycus is a human being who possesses playful powers and who until now has believed he was fully in charge of his own destiny. But within his time on stage he discovers, despite his efforts to remain a knave, that he is not fully his own master. Autolycus becomes an instrument in providential discoveries and restorations beyond his knowledge or his intention.

Perdita and Florizel move us profoundly when they speak Shakespeare's most beautiful love poetry. Although Perdita may long for an Edenic nature in which no disguises are employed and no art allowed, she and Florizel play at both mythological and artful pastoral disguises. Like many of Shakespeare's heroines, Perdita shows no coyness in her declarations of love. She and Florizel dream of a mutual, true, and eternal love, and they are as firmly committed to their dream and to each other as Paulina is to Hermione, or, in the first part of the play, Leontes to his malign illusion. Florizel's love almost leads him to the most dangerous possibility of adoration: the attempt to stop time, to freeze the moment, to transform his living loved one into an icon; but his wishes change even as she changes:

> What you do,
> Still betters what is done. When you speak, sweet,
> I'd have you do it ever: when you sing
> I'd have you buy and sell so, so give alms,
> Pray so, and, for the ord'ring your affairs,
> To sing them too: when you do dance, I wish you
> A wave o' th' sea, that you might ever do
> Nothing but that, move still, still so,
> And own no other function. Each your doing,
> So singular in each particular,
> Crowns what you are doing, in the present deeds,
> That all your acts are queens.   (IV. iv. 135-46)

The present, moving Perdita always remains the object of Florizel's desires. Their love triumphs both within time and against time. Perdita admits that poverty and misadventure may certainly change her body, but she is convinced that they cannot change her love; and Florizel insists that his faith and love can never fail while the world exists.[17] Beyond their verbal commitments, the actions and responses of Florizel and Perdita amid festivities and threats and dangers help convince us that theirs is indeed a true love, 'something of great constancy; / But howsoever, strange and admirable'.[18]

Shakespeare avoids direct presentation of the first big, expected scene of discovery and reconciliation. Instead we, along with Autolycus, hear a group of courtly (and largely anonymous) gentlemen piece out both the events and their admiration, disbelief, and wonder. They use a great many words to describe how far the events and the emotions aroused by them went beyond words:

First Gentleman. I make a broken delivery of the business; but the changes I perceived in the king and Camillo were very notes of admiration: they seemed almost, with staring on one another, to tear the cases of their eyes: there was speech in their dumbness, language in their very gesture; they looked as they had heard of a world ransomed, or one destroyed: a notable passion of wonder appeared in them; but the wisest beholder, that knew no more but seeing, could not say if th' importance were joy or sorrow; but in the extremity of the one it must needs be. . . .

Second Gentleman. This news, which is called true, is so like an old tale that the verity of it is in strong suspicion.   (V. ii. 9-29)

Third Gentleman. Did you see the meeting of the two kings?
Second Gentleman. No.
Third Gentleman. Then have you lost a sight which was to be seen, cannot be spoken of.   (V. ii. 40-4)

They have become connoisseurs of aesthetic effects of admiration or wonder—judges, even, of the proper relations between actors and audiences:

First Gentleman. The dignity of this act was worth the audience of kings and princes; for by such was it acted.
Third Gentleman. One of the prettiest touches of all, and that which angled for mine eyes (caught the water though not the fish) was, when at the relation of the queen's death (with the manner how she came to

---

17 Florizel's oath (IV. iv. 477-80) has some resemblance to Lear's in *King Lear* III. ii. 6-9. Lear, however, is convinced that corruption and ingratitude have triumphed in this world and he wishes all life to stop; Florizel is so sure of the strength and durability of his love that all nature might as well die if it should fail.

18 *A Midsummer Night's Dream*, V. i. 26-7.

't bravely confessed and lamented by the king) how attentiveness wounded his daughter; till, from one sign of dolour to another, she did, with an 'Alas,' I would fain say, bleed tears, for I am sure my heart wept blood. Who was most marble, there changed colour; some swooned, all sorrowed: if all the world could have seen 't, the woe had been universal.   (V. ii. 79-91)

We wish to go off immediately with these gentlemen to see Paulina's statue of Hermione, since 'Who would be thence that has the benefit of access? Every wink of an eye, some new grace will be born: our absence makes us unthrifty to our knowledge' (V. ii. 109-12). But we are teasingly delayed by Autolycus and his encounter with the newly genteel Clown and Shepherd; that delay, even with its laughter, sharpens our anticipation. We have heard repeatedly the notion that sight may overwhelmingly convince us of marvellous possibilities which the ear alone would reject as unbelievable, and we look forward to a moving spectacle of wonder. The confident dramatist has dared to make his audience anticipate a miracle; and in one of the most astonishingly effective scenes he ever created for the theatre, Shakespeare does not disappoint them.

Revelations of falsity, betrayal, loss, destruction, and death are frequently credible upon mere report—often enough we find them even predictable. What we need to *see* to believe are evidences of truth, faith, recovery and renewal, new creation, love—those things which we can never reliably predict, and which, seemingly, we never quite deserve. We would certainly be unlikely to believe the mere relation of the awakening to life of a figure we thought we knew was dead—particularly when our supposed knowledge had been substantiated by the appearance of the ghost of the deceased.[19] But we cannot doubt the play's final vision of the 'statue' and the long process of slow awakening, both of the faith of all the spectators on and off stage and of the central figure to movement and speech. The first response of all to the unveiling of the statue is silence. It is only after Paulina comments on the silence that Leontes first addresses the 'dear stone' as if it were alive and then complains

_____

[19] The sceptical Antigonus's description in III. ii. 16-46 of the supposed ghost of Hermione helps to confirm our conviction of her death—despite the fact that he interprets that appearance as confirmation of her guilt.

to Paulina that this figure is older and much more wrinkled
than the young, lost queen. Perdita breaks her silence to kneel
for a blessing and ask the figure to extend her hand to kiss: after
the initial wonder the pressures continually increase for the
figure to become more than a motionless object of vision.
When Paulina starts to draw the curtain 'lest your fancy / May
think anon it moves' (V. iii. 60-1) or even lives, Leontes exclaims:

> O sweet Paulina,
> Make me to think so twenty years together!
> No settled senses of the world can match
> The pleasure of that madness. Let 't alone.
> (70-5)

Few of us would prefer 'settled senses' to that sort of madness.
   After Paulina prevents Leontes from kissing the figure, she
warns him,

> Either forbear,
> Quit presently the chapel, or resolve you
> For more amazement. If you can behold it,
> I'll make the statue move indeed; descend,
> And take you by the hand: but then you'll think
> (Which I protest against) I am assisted
> By wicked powers.   (85-91)

Leontes never hesitates. He is sure that his dream is single: the
full recovery of his lost love—image, movement, and voice:

> What you can make her do,
> I am content to look on: what to speak,
> I am content to hear; for 'tis as easy
> To make her speak as move.   (91-4)

Paulina responds with a double warning, seemingly addressed
to the audience off stage as well as on:

> It is requir'd
> You do awake your faith. Then all stand still:
> On:20 those that think it is unlawful business
> I am about, let them depart.   (94-7)

---

20 I retain the Folio's *On* and colon instead of following Hanmer's and Pafford's
emendation to *Or* and dash.

Leontes resumes the imperative of his royal manner: 'Proceed: / No foot shall stir' (97-8). But Paulina uses even more
imperatives as she openly assumes her role of good and powerful magician. Her language, assisted by the music so often
present at the most intense moments of the plays, focuses our
attention on the essential meanings inherent in the visible
movements on stage:

>   Music, awake her; strike! [*Music*]
> 'Tis time; descend; be stone no more; approach;
> Strike all that look upon with marvel. Come!
> I'll fill your grave up: stir, nay, come away:
> Bequeath to death your numbness; for from him
> Dear life redeems you. You perceive she stirs:
>   [*Hermione comes down*]
> Start not; her actions shall be holy as
> You hear my spell is lawful. [*To Leontes*] Do not shun her
> Until you see her die again; for then
> You kill her double. Nay, present your hand:
> When she was young you woo'd her; now, in age,
> Is she become the suitor?   (98-109)

With their inevitable embrace, Leontes exclaims at the discovery that the extended suffering and the intricate artifice that
he and we have experienced and witnessed have returned us to
the waking world of flesh and blood:

>   O, she's warm!
> If this be magic, let it be an art
> Lawful as eating.   (109-11)

Hermione's and Paulina's dreams of the vindication of Hermione's honour and of Leontes' sorrow and repentance and
recovery of his love have been fulfilled; but Hermione finally
speaks only when she asks the gods' blessings upon her lost
daughter. It was the hope of Perdita's recovery that had made
Hermione 'preserve' herself during those intervening years.

Some readers have complained at the speedy contrivance by
which Leontes, in the closing lines of the play, neatly pairs off
Paulina and Camillo (seemingly to their surprise), so that the
rejoicing in new and old wedded love may be fully shared by
all. But in the theatre, the arbitrariness is overwhelmed by the
comedy. Paulina, who has said so much, first as a moral scold

and later as the wary mistress of Leontes' repentance, insists even in the midst of congratulating the others that, rather than continuing to share in the general joy, she will spend the rest of her life in lamentation for her lost Antigonus:

> Go together
> You precious winners all; your exultation
> Partake to every one. I, an old turtle,
> Will wing me to some wither'd bough, and there
> My mate (that's never to be found again)
> Lament, till I am lost.   (130-5)

She seems to want to make sure that no one will forget that *she* is not one of the 'winners'; however pleased at the happy fulfilment of all her plans, she wants them to notice that she is not dancing at the wedding. Unless the actor who plays Leontes works hard to prevent them, the audience laughs at his response, 'O, peace, Paulina!'—a sentiment as long delayed and almost as much desired as Albany's response to Goneril, 'Shut your mouth, dame', near the end of *King Lear* (V. iii. 154). His plan for the unexpected marriage seems to promise that Paulina can once again learn to enjoy modes of speech beyond shrewish or mournful accusations and complaints, or even magisterial and magical revelations.

We are spared the inevitably anticlimactic explanation, but there is one more touching recollection of the beginning of the play, when sight did not provide sure revelation of truth. Despite their recent reconciliation and joy, Leontes suddenly notices that Hermione, whose warm and courteous glances he had once so disastrously misinterpreted as those of adulterous passion, refuses now to look at Polixenes:

> What! look upon my brother: both your pardons
> That e'er I put between your holy looks
> My ill suspicion.   (147-9)

If they will look at each other again (as they surely now do), they will show that they truly have faith that Leontes' understanding has been restored along with his love, that they trust him as well as forgive him. Amid all the rejoicings of the happy ending, those lines suggest that the tensions and changes of life continue.

Ordinarily we dream of persons, actions, predicaments, things, rather than directly of meanings or significances. In *A Midsummer Night's Dream* the dreams were primarily of young lovers, moonlight, madness, and illusions, and the happy endings concerned the discovery of true love in the seemingly timeless world sometimes available to the young and the lucky. At the end of *The Winter's Tale*, as in our happiest dreams, we are no longer anxious about either power or time because we have imaginatively experienced their destructive possibilities and we have truly come to know our loves and to understand their languages.

III

The Dream of a Hero: *Hamlet*

Most commentaries on Shakespeare's *The Tragedy of Hamlet, Prince of Denmark* end, even if they do not begin, with talking about the central character of the play as if he were a living human being with real, non-theatrical problems. Shakespeare has created a world and a character so dense and various, in language so evocative and rich, that both world and character insistently leave the stage and enter our imaginations and our ordinary lives. The temptation to consider Hamlet's character and personality as well as his actions as 'real' events which we must try to understand and evaluate is so strong that it is difficult to resist it. (I shall undoubtedly succumb before I complete this essay.) In the long run, some may think it hardly to the point even to try. If one accepts John Bayley's beguiling arguments[1] that the literary characters we come truly to love are likely to be those whom their creators have also come to love in the very act of creation, and that the emotions both author and reader or viewer come to feel are inevitably in excess of the supposed architectonic necessities of the works within which those characters find their lives, then we may simply recognize that, for most readers and viewers for almost four centuries, Hamlet is one of the supreme characters of love—however much some commentators from the eighteenth century until today have found to lament in his personality and his behaviour.[2]

Nevertheless, I think it is worth the effort to try to focus, at least initially, on Hamlet as a figure in a play; for the great disadvantage in proceeding directly to a consideration of Hamlet's personality or morality is that those who do so usually focus immediately on what is *wrong* with Hamlet. Perhaps it is

---

[1] John Bayley, *The Characters of Love: A Study in the Literature of Personality* (London, 1960).

[2] G. K. Hunter has remarked of Othello, 'I fear that one has to be trained as a literary critic to find him unadmirable' (*Dramatic Identities and Cultural Traditions: Studies in Shakespeare and His Contemporaries*, New York, 1978, p. 59). I believe one could say much the same thing about Hamlet.

because we want some sort of happy ending for the characters we are tempted to like—or even to love; we are certainly likely to feel dissatisfied if they should die unmarried, killed by the evil forces they have opposed, never having been 'put on' in the responsibilities of power. We are particularly likely to feel threatened by the tragic or wasteful death of an individual if our love for him has been partly based upon, or has led to, an unusual degree of personal identification. To such a dramatic situation, some will respond by concentrating on those characteristics or attributes of the figure that they or their cultures particularly condemn, so as to establish a distance from the threatening identification. (And so eighteenth-century critics, like some modern ones, have concentrated on Hamlet's passionate nature or instability, his failures at rational control, his impolite and even cruel language to Ophelia and Gertrude, or the bloodthirstiness or impiety of his sentiments with the kneeling Claudius, etc.) Others may accept fully their sense of personal identification with the unfulfilled hero and take comfort in emphasizing the analogous weaknesses or failures that prevent their own potential heroism from achieving fulfilment. (And so from the early nineteenth century there is the characteristic emphasis on Hamlet's over-intellectualism, his too exquisite sensibility, his paralysing melancholy, and his supposed incapacity for action.) Although in the twentieth century critics' attempts both to distance and to accept their sense of identification with Hamlet have often uneasily coexisted, the efforts to distance seem to predominate as they have explored Hamlet's supposedly unrelieved Oedipal conflict (with tragedy sadly inevitable without proper modern diagnosis and treatment) or Hamlet's moral or theological errors, particularly his ignorance of the properly Christian attitudes towards the taking of revenge and the nature of ghosts. Harold Skulsky was unusual only in the intensity of his judgements when he denounced Hamlet's 'gullibility', his 'failure of logic and imagination', lack of 'compassion and equity', and 'shallow competitiveness': 'The theme of Hamlet's development, or rather disclosure, is intellectual talent debauched in the service of intellectual vanity, and of mindless activism. Given the theme, his final self-indulgence is what one might expect: a retreat from deliberate choice to that notorious *asylum stultorum*, divine Providence.'[3]

In our dreams or folklore or theatres, we ordinarily desire for a supremely gifted figure both a triumphant display of his power and a happy ending: a lover who wins the girl, a master of wit and action who wins the battles of both the head and the heart, a soldier who triumphs in battle, the prince who slays the dragon or breaks the charm or wins the proper princess, a king who saves the state and rules with justice. When a figure promising such triumphs is created with remarkable reality and then loses love and power and life, we find it almost unbearable. If the figure is in a play, we may begin to write as if the proper object of dramatic criticism were to explain how tragedy might have been—indeed, *should* have been—avoided. At that point, we have surely moved too far from our experience of the play that was written for a theatre.

If we return to the theatre and its, at least imaginary, stage, we may become less interested in trying to determine what is wrong either with Hamlet or *Hamlet* (we may, as a matter of fact, see very little wrong with the character and nothing at all with the great dramatic construction), and become more interested in trying to discover how we get our impressions of the most vital presence we have known in the theatre and how we come to love him. In the latter process, we may become increasingly sceptical about the truth of those favourite Elizabethan analogies between the stage and the world. For whatever the architecture of the Globe Theatre and whatever we may think or feel during a fine performance of a first-rate play, theatrical excellence and human or moral excellence are rarely simply identical: we often admire actions on stage which would horrify us off stage, and we might well find the dramatic imitation of the highest moral virtue theatrically stupefying. If happy families are all alike and therefore do not provide the subjects for our most interesting novels, happy individuals are even less likely to provide the central figures for our most compelling dramas—those that include full recognition of power and evil and death as well as love. Although some of our difficulties with *Hamlet* may derive from the fact that Shakespeare did so much

---

[3] *Spirits Finely Touched: The Testing of Value and Integrity in Four Shakespearean Plays* (Athens, Ga., 1976), pp. 37-8, 51, 79-80.

to make his central figure morally admirable, the dramatist may have begun with a simpler aim: the creation of a central figure who combined and demonstrated almost all the abilities and characteristics that had proved most attractive on stage in his former masculine central figures, whether lovers, soldiers, masters of wit, kings or princes, heroes, or moralists. For the sources of the dramatic figure of Hamlet, we should not look exclusively to the earlier versions of the Hamlet legend or to earlier or contemporary revenge plays by Kyd or others, but to Shakespeare's own earlier or contemporary histories and comedies and tragedies.[4]

Whatever the genres, all those central, young masculine figures initially seem to belong to the category that Harriett Hawkins has labelled 'winners' rather than 'losers'.[5] They are heroes or potential heroes, and they show unusual daring, agility, and physical strength. They frequently demonstrate their knowledge and skill in martial arts, and even inauspicious victories, such as Romeo's over Tybalt, may furnish validation of their heroic status. However lacking in reputation or unprepossessing in appearance, they nearly always win, even if the contested event is as socially ignoble as Orlando's wrestling match. In the histories, so frequently concerned with flawed kings and princes and questions of succession, the central figures may be morally dubious or even reprehensible, but they are marvellously stage-worthy: that compelling figure Richard III is not only clever and powerful and imaginatively evil, but he is also brave and frequently victorious on the battlefield; Richmond must prove his right by conquering him in single combat. Bolingbroke is quick to challenge Mowbray to combat, and he is effective as warrior as well as politician. Hotspur's military valour causes others besides Henry IV to consider him the true heir to the throne; and Hal must prove

---

[4] Anne Barton has anticipated my point in her introduction to the New Penguin edition of *Hamlet*, ed. T. J. B. Spencer (Harmondsworth, 1980), p. 18: 'Certainly it [*Hamlet*] seems more than any other play he wrote to provide a kind of retrospect on his previous work, gathering to itself many of the themes and preoccupations of the tragedies, histories, and comedies he had already produced. There is a sense in which they, quite as much as the *Ur-Hamlet* provided a basis for Shakespeare's *Hamlet*.'

[5] 'Poetic Injustice: Some Winners and Losers in Medieval and Renaissance Literature', *Poetic Freedom and Poetic Truth: Chaucer, Shakespeare, Marlowe, Milton* (Oxford, 1976), pp. 1-25.

his identity as Prince of Wales by giving the gallant Hotspur his mortal wound upon the battlefield. Prowess and willingness to venture with the sword are such essential characteristics of the heroic stage-figure that, as with Sebastian in *Twelfth Night* (a play that may come shortly after *Hamlet* in the Shakespeare canon), they may provide important clues to his recognition.

Although sometimes missing from romantic productions, such physical and military bravery and skill are also signal characteristics of Hamlet. They are evidenced repeatedly from the moment when he dares to follow the Ghost and threatens the restraining Horatio and Marcellus with his sword ('Unhand me, gentlemen. / By heaven, I'll make a ghost of him that lets me. / I say away'—I. iv. 84-6), until he wins the first two hits in the match with Laertes, skilfully exchanges swords and wounds his opponent, stabs the King after he learns that his mother was poisoned and his sword's point envenomed, forces Claudius to drink the dregs of the cup, and then, almost unbelievably, uses his dying strength to struggle with Horatio and force him to give up the cup:

> As th'art a man
> Give me the cup. Let go, by Heaven, I'll ha't.
> (V. ii. 347-8)

In between we see him stabbing Polonius through the arras, hear of his boarding the pirate ship during the sea battle, see him leaping into Ophelia's grave and grappling with Laertes. Hamlet's physical energy and daring would be difficult to exaggerate. Only he and the Ghost ever cast any doubts on his bravery or sense of purpose, and they both also fear that his passionate commitment to action and his excitement might lead him to kill Gertrude.

Aside from physical energy, strength, agility, mastery, the other most obvious way in which a stage character can dominate the Shakespearian (or any other) stage is through verbal energy, inventiveness, and mastery. As early as *Love's Labour's Lost* one can recognize immediately that Berowne, not the King of Navarre, is the central figure because he is the wittiest man on stage. He can argue convincingly on almost any side of any issue, he thoroughly enjoys his own and others' inventions and absurdities, and he can change his language instantly with every changing situation or nuance. (If he nevertheless is bested by Rosaline, we simply recognize that in Shakespearian comedy verbal combats of wit are the only ones that young heroic gentlemen may frequently lose, without disgrace, to their even wittier ladies.) Berowne is recognizably related to Mercutio: their quicksilver wit is a family characteristic almost guaranteed to dominate any scene in which it is given a chance for display. It is associated with mercurial emotions, a taste for improvisation, self-dramatization, disguises and verbal games, a frequently sceptical or unillusioned stance, and some gift for bawdry. When the witty hero is forced, like both Berowne and Benedick, to recognize his own vulnerability to irrational forces beyond his control, his soliloquies can be very funny.[6]

Heroes of histories and tragedies as well as comedies frequently display their verbal mastery. Before his gallant death, Richard II largely dominates his stage by the sole means of his imaginative verbal inventions; but it is Richard's weakness that he can hardly imagine a scene, linguistic or political, of which he is not the recognized centre. He lacks exactly the flexibility and sceptical suspicion of grandiose language that promise better things for Berowne and Benedick as well as for a royal Henry IV and Hal. That Richard is ultimately a failed hero, in the rising light of Bolingbroke, is conveyed by his confusion of language with external physical and social reality, his trust that words alone may transform things.

Prince Hal, particularly in *Henry IV, Part I*, is the single figure before *Hamlet* who most completely combines the peculiar gifts of both the stage hero and not only the ideal, but also the successful, prince. As we follow his education (or, more accurately, the scenic unfolding of his physical, linguistic, intellectual, and emotional range), we recognize his energy, his playfulness, his insatiable curiosity, his ingenuity, and, most important of all, his ability to respond almost instantaneously to changes in the world around him, to recognize new opportunities and necessities, to judge them, and to act upon them. At the beginning something of a male Cinderella (even if we know nothing of the historical figure, his father's initial un-

---

[6] See, for example, Berowne's soliloquy in *Love's Labour's Lost*, III. i. 168-200, and Benedick's in *Much Ado About Nothing*, II. iii. 211-37.

paternal sentiments predispose us in his favour before we ever see him), Hal is surrounded in the play by any number of rival or alternative models of a true prince, both living and ghostly: the aged presence and remembered youth of his politic father; the memory of Richard II; the nobly romantic Edmund Mortimer, whose hereditary claim to the throne may be sounder than Hal's; his own younger brother, Prince John of Lancaster, well-regarded, responsible, and brave; the foreign possibilities of brave Douglas and powerful and mysterious Glendower; and above all, the gallant Hotspur. There are a few moments, however, when the qualities are fully demonstrated or revealed that make Hal's claims dramatically undeniable: the scenes with his father, the magnanimous final moment when he gives Prince John the largesse of granting Douglas's freedom, and, supremely, his battle with, and defeat of, Hotspur. Lawrence Ross[7] has suggested that when Hal stands above the bodies of the dead Hotspur and the shamming Falstaff, he is revealed as the true heir of both, or even the 'new man' come miraculously alive from the ruined corruptions of both that linguistically gifted, outrageously witty, charming, immoral, and cowardly old man and that militarily gifted, gallant, hot-tempered, and hopelessly impolitic younger one. Hal seems to have inherited the virtues and gifts of both these strange fathers without their vices or weaknesses. In the subsequent plays, moreover, he demonstrates that he knows as well as his natural father how to gain power—and even better how to keep it. Of course the fact that he has inherited rather than usurped a throne relieves him of the burden of his father's remorse of conscience; but Hal is also remarkably successful at shifting the moral problems that do remain and that subsequently arise to the broad shoulders of the Church, the national interest, and the laws of war. Before he succeeds to rule, Hal realizes fully what Richard II never understood: that in a prosperous and stable kingdom something like justice must not only be done but must also be seen to be done; and so he recognizes that, with his assumption of power, Falstaff must go.

---

[7] *Wingless Victory: Michelangelo, Shakespeare, and the 'Old Man'*, University of Wisconsin Literary Monographs, 2 (Madison, 1969).

We seem to have come quite a distance from Hal's linguistic mastery and its anticipation of Hamlet's. Yet one cannot say much about linguistic ability without relating it to other qualities: imagination, intelligence, the speaker's relations to others, his capacity for emotion, for commitment, and for judgement. Mercutio's inventiveness and exuberance, for example, function within a relatively narrow range; Romeo, by contrast, establishes his central dramatic importance in his rapid development from the melancholy victim of love-in-idleness to a seemingly much older figure capable of imaginative sympathy, tenderness, and resolution as well as witty artifice, passionate love, and passionate despair. It is Hal who comes closest to anticipating Hamlet's combination of extraordinary physical and verbal mastery with an even more unusual emotional, imaginative, and social range. The Hal who delighted in learning the specialized and limited language of Francis the Drawer at the Boar's Head looks forward to the Hamlet who delights in the language of the gravediggers. Hotspur is infuriated by the foppish 'popinjay' who demands his prisoners; but Hamlet is delighted with that courtier's cousin, Osric, insists on understanding every one of his outrageous terms (Horatio remarks, 'I knew you must be edified by the margin ere you had done'—V. ii. 152-3), and finally outdoes and baffles him with his own brand of extravagant and strained language. Hal's styles, both as young prince and later as King Henry V, range widely: from his language with Falstaff and Poins and the rest at the Boar's Head to his language with his father; from his challenge to Hotspur to his elegy for him; from his speeches to the bishops to those with the traitors; from those in his own person to the English troops to those in disguise to Fluellen, Gower, John Bates, and Michael Williams; from the addresses to the French lords before battle to the badinage with the French princess. Often that range is directly related to his delight and success in planning and carrying out an elaborate scene: in the charade at Gad's Hill; the episode with Francis; the comic rehearsals with Falstaff and the very different scene when he actually meets his father; his meeting with Hotspur on the battlefield; his theatrical treatment of Scroop, Cambridge, and Gray; the effective scene with the soldiers when he is disguised in Sir Thomas Erpingham's cloak; the heroic charges into battle; the charade with Williams and the gloves; the successful courtship of Princess Katherine in *franglais*.

But all this only anticipates Hamlet's even more extraordinary range of language—wider by far than that of any other character in the plays of Shakespeare or in any other plays I know. It is not only a matter of the distance between his inward (or sometimes histrionic) soliloquies and, say, his courtly cordiality when he first meets Rosencrantz and Guildenstern, between his ironic baiting of Claudius and his impassioned accusations of Gertrude, between the 'mad' language he speaks to Polonius and the 'mad' language he speaks to Ophelia, the directness of most of his speeches to Horatio and the doggerel to which he dances after the play scene: the shifts in tone within a single scene or even within a single speech are frequently as astonishing. David Young has described the way in which, at his first meeting with his father's ghost, Hamlet 'manages both to be enormously respectful and astonishingly disrespectful':[8] from 'King, father, royal Dane' (I. iv. 45) to 'Art thou there, truepenny?' and 'this fellow in the cellarage' (I. v. 158-9). Other memorable shifts are from 'Nay, but to live / In the rank sweat of an enseamed bed, / Stew'd in corruption, honeying and making love / Over the nasty sty!' to 'And when you are desirous to be blest, / I'll blessing beg of you', and 'Good night, mother' (III. iv. 91-4, 173-4, 219); from 'Bloody, bawdy villain! / Remorseless, treacherous, lecherous, kindless villain!' to the following line, 'Why, what an ass am I!' (II. ii. 576-8); from his 'by Heaven, I'll ha't' to Horatio to 'Absent thee from felicity awhile' (V. ii. 348, 352).

The business of an actor is to act. *Hamlet* gives the actor who plays the title role more continuous opportunities (they are really demands) to dominate the stage than any other Shakespeare play gives to any other actor. Of the play's twenty scenes, as usually printed, the character Hamlet clearly dominates ten.[9] And in other scenes descriptions of Hamlet (as in

---

[8] '*Hamlet* Son of *Hamlet*', *Perspectives on Hamlet*, ed. William G. Holzberger and Peter B. Waldeck (Lewisburg and London, 1975), p. 196.

[9] Although there may be disagreements of interpretation, I believe that most actors and readers will usually agree on which scenes 'belong to' which character on the basis of the number of lines he speaks, the intensity or dramatic effectiveness of those lines, and whether he is dominant at the end of the scene. In complex or episodic scenes, the judgement will probably be based largely on which character dominates the larger number of episodes.

I. iii) or letters from him (as in IV. vi) threaten the domination of the characters to whom they primarily belong. Claudius, Hamlet's 'mighty opposite', is the only character in the play whose dramatic importance can even be compared with Hamlet's; but his dominance is frequently threatened within the six scenes that are chiefly his. In Act IV, scene vii, for example, Claudius's skilful manipulation of Laertes is interrupted by the unexpected, and stylistically impertinent, threatening letter from Hamlet, and then dramatically upstaged by Gertrude's description of Ophelia's death and by Laertes' grief: at his exit, Claudius does not lead but follows Laertes because he fears that those events will undo his hard-won control over Laertes' will.

But Hamlet's domination of the stage and his heroic stature are not merely matters of his physical daring, his energy, his flexibility, his linguistic range, or his intelligence. (He impresses most viewers as the most intelligent human character ever presented in the theatre.) His emotions, also, are as quick and as intense as his perceptions and his shifts in tone or role—from a melancholy near despair, scorn, disgust, hatred, to sympathy, tenderness, amusement, playfulness, and excited anticipation. The range is so extreme that, among other amateur psychiatric diagnoses,[10] he has been thought to suffer from manic-depression. But whatever our judgements concerning mature and well-adjusted personalities at home or at work, most of us prefer on stage an emotional quality even Hamlet recognizes as occasionally extravagant ('Something too much of this', he remarks of his own enthusiastic approval of the Horatio he sees as superior to the 'buffets and rewards' of Fortune—III. ii. 74) to the sort of emotional control (or even apathy) usually displayed by Horatio and admired by the neo-Stoics[11] and many modern moralists. Attempts to present a completely controlled character as the central figure in a drama are likely to make most members of an audience echo Roy Campbell's complaint

[10] Any psychiatric diagnosis of a *literary* character, even if it is made by Freud or Jones or any other psychiatrist, can only be 'amateur', since the subject does not live apart from the imaginations of his creator, his interpreters, and his audience, and the patient is unavailable for questioning or therapy.

[11] G. K. Hunter has remarked, 'Not only in contrast with Horatio (though most obviously there) but throughout the play, Hamlet seems almost deliberately designed as a counterblast to the received figure of the Christian-Stoic hero' ('The Heroism of Hamlet', *Dramatic Identities and Cultural Traditions*, p. 242).

'On Some South African Novelists': 'They use the snaffle and the curb all right, / But where's the bloody horse?'[12]

It is Hamlet's glory that he is not superior to feeling; he is as alert to its nuances within himself as within others. He exposes and even exaggerates both his own responses and his flaws or failures of feeling as well as action, analyses them so thoroughly that he has anticipated almost every hostile criticism that can be made of him. He suffers greatly (in his capacity for suffering he is nearer to Lear than to any other tragic protagonist in Shakespeare's plays): in his initial isolated mourning at court, with the Ghost, in his farewell to Ophelia, in hearing the player's speech of Hecuba, in his farewell to Gertrude, in his struggles to become a 'proper' avenger. He also demonstrates what seems to be a natural capacity for enjoyment and play: in greeting Horatio and Rosencrantz and Guildenstern, with the players, with the gravediggers, with Osric, in imagining the 'sport' of hoisting an 'enginer' with his own 'petard', in taunting Claudius at his farewell 'for England', even initially in his fencing match with Laertes. He shows, too, his capacity for love: for his father, for Gertrude, for Ophelia, for Horatio. He has nothing of the single-minded and frequently humourless pursuit of limited goals that characterizes a number of Shakespeare's villains (Iago and Claudius, for example), questionable figures such as Bolingbroke or the Caesar of *Antony and Cleopatra*, or an absurd comic figure such as Malvolio. It is exactly this lack of serious single-mindedness which causes Claudius to speak of him contemptuously as 'Most generous, and free from all contriving' (IV. vii. 134), and which guarantees the sympathies of most of those members of the audience who do not intuitively sympathize with seriously striving egoists or who have not been taught better on theological or moral grounds. As alertly concious of his 'self' as anyone we can imagine, Hamlet yet persuades us that he is capable of forgetting himself in his astonishing zest for life. Seeking, and occasionally seeming to unite, the primary gifts of passion, wisdom, and power,[13] the notoriously divided Hamlet centrally affirms decency and wholeness.

[12] *The Oxford Book of Twentieth-Century English Verse*, ed. Philip Larkin (Oxford, 1973), No. 312.

[13] Cf. Nigel Alexander, *Passion, Play, and Duel: A Study in Hamlet* (London, 1971), pp. 131-9.

But this Hamlet, seemingly a supreme example of a heroic winner, loses—or, more accurately, he loses his chance for a united and loving family, fulfilled sexual love, the chance to serve openly as a soldier or to succeed to royal power, the chance of a long life. He wins what, after the graveyard scene, both he and we may come to see as more important: the bringing to light of hidden crimes, the purging of the state, the final forgiveness of Laertes and the final loyalty of his mother, public recognition as a brave soldier who became an honourable casualty in an undeclared war.

A number (although from the record, apparently a minority) of twentieth-century scholars and critics[14] have recognized that the causes of the losses, the things that make Hamlet a *tragic* hero, do not stem primarily from supposed weaknesses or flaws in Hamlet's character or even mistakes in his judgement or actions, but from the evil and intolerable situation in which he finds himself. Upon the death of his loved and heroic father, the prince discovers that his uncle is elected king and that his mother, rather than mourning for her dead husband the customary amount of time, marries her former brother-in-law (incestuously, but with the approval of the court) so quickly as to cause inevitable suspicion that she had betrayed her husband before his death.[15] When his uncle, the new king, will not allow

[14] The distinguished roll of those who have written memorably on the subject includes, among many others, E. E. Stoll (particularly *Hamlet: An Historical and Comparative Study*, Minneapolis, 1919, and *Hamlet the Man*, London, 1935), Peter Alexander (*Shakespeare's Life and Art*, London, 1939, and *Hamlet: Father and Son*, Oxford, 1955, Helen Gardner ('The Historical Approach', *The Business of Criticism*, Oxford, 1959, pp. 35-51), Madeleine Doran ('The Language of *Hamlet*', *Huntington Library Quarterly*, 27 (1963-4), 259-78; essentially reprinted as ' "No art at all" Language in *Hamlet*', *Shakespeare's Dramatic Language*, Madison, 1976, pp. 32-62), G. K. Hunter ('The Heroism of Hamlet', *Hamlet*, Stratford-upon-Avon Studies, 5, ed. J. R. Brown and B. Harris, London, 1963, pp. 90-109; reprinted in *Dramatic Identities and Cultural Traditions*, pp. 230-50), Maurice Charney (*Style in 'Hamlet'*, Princeton, 1969), Nigel Alexander (*Passion, Play, and Duel*, 1971), and E. A. J. Honigmann ('Hamlet as Observer and Consciousness', *Shakespeare: Seven Tragedies: The Dramatist's Manipulation of Response*, New York, 1976, pp. 54-66). Maynard Mack's influential essay, 'The World of Hamlet' (*Yale Review*, 41 (1952), 502-23), emphasizes the flaws and failures of the hero, and Harry Levin's brilliant *The Question of 'Hamlet'* (New York, 1959) makes a persuasive case for the play as the chief masterpiece of indeterminacy. I am personally indebted to an essay by Barbara Deming that takes a middle ground: 'The World of Hamlet', *Tulane Drama Review*, 4 (1959), 36-44.

[15] Roland Frye tells of a commencement address at the University of Pennsylvania where Art Buchwald told of an undergraduate who, when asked how he would respond if he came home from college and discovered that his father had died suddenly

him to return to his life as a student in Wittenberg, Hamlet, in his grief and anger,[16] initially wishes to die because there seems to be no honourable way in which he can act either to relieve his emotions or to defend his father's name; when he hears reports of the appearance of his father's ghost he is both relieved and excited. When the ghost tells of his suffering, confirms the suspicions of Gertrude's adultery, reveals that Claudius secretly murdered him, and demands that Hamlet should both 'Revenge his foul and most unnatural murder' (I. v. 25) and also 'Let not the royal bed of Denmark be / A couch for luxury and damned incest' (I. v. 82-3), Hamlet is momentarily exuberant at the opportunity for purposeful action; but within less than eighty lines, he has recognized the fatal burden of the supernatural behest:

> The time is out of joint. O cursed spite,
> That ever I was born to set it right.
> (I. v. 196-7)

Hamlet is imaginative as well as intelligent. Within those few moments, he has recognized that revenge must be a task he undertakes privately and secretly (there is no possible proof of the murder, and the state has both crowned Claudius and accepted his marriage), that it will mean the abandonment of any hopes he may have had for love and marriage (what intelligent hero capable of feeling could plan for domestic felicity while plotting a vengeful killing that will appear treasonous?), and that even if he succeeds rather than dies in his attempted vengeance, it will mean the destruction of his mother's present happiness and probably her final separation from him. Later, when he questions the ghost's origins and veracity, he sensibly determines to secure more substantial evidence of Claudius's guilt.

Hamlet's predicament comes close to the ultimate tragic situation in both Greek drama and northern European legend, when differing moral absolutes, with their concomitant imperatives to action, come into direct opposition. The unheroic

under mysterious circumstances, his mother had married his uncle within six weeks of her husband's death, and his uncle had taken over his father's business, unconsciously echoed Hamlet's initial response with, 'I think I'd go for an MA.'

16 See Arthur Kirsch, 'Hamlet's Grief', *ELH* 48 (1981), 17-36.

Chorus in Sophocles' *Antigone* comes belatedly to recognize such a situation only when, just after they have reiterated the conventional position that they will be friends to no one who does not honour both the laws of the gods and the laws of the state, they see Antigone brought on in chains: they are horrified to recognize that at this moment the laws of the state are directly opposed to the laws of the gods (and of familial love) and that for a heroic Antigone and their own society there can be no escaping death and tragic loss. Orestes *must* avenge Agamemnon's death; but his bloody murders of Aegisthus and Clytemnestra entail almost unbelievable suffering for him, and it is only divine intervention that at last transforms the avenging Erynyes into the grateful Eumenides.[17] A member of a Germanic *comitatus* owed absolute military and personal devotion both to his leader and to his own family; suffering and death must inevitably result when an individual hero's family was betrayed or dishonoured by his leader. Since the most sacred masculine relationship in Celtic legend was between maternal uncle and nephew, only tragedy could result if that relationship was poisoned by incest: the birth of Mordred, both son and nephew of Arthur, inevitably foreshadowed the destruction of the Round Table and the death of Arthur.

Within medieval and Renaissance societies, the duty to avenge familial murders and acts of dishonour was frequently in direct conflict with the Christian imperative to forgive one's enemies and with the civic laws against private vengeance. In most Renaissance plays, assumption of the revenger's role almost inevitably resulted in the moral debasement and physical destruction of the avenger in the process of accomplishing his revenge. Anne Barton has remarked that within the theatre we ordinarily begin to feel alienated from the revenger the moment he decides to kill:

Only in Shakespeare's *Hamlet* does the audience retain sympathy for the hero from beginning to end. This is no mean dramaturgical feat, considering that Hamlet is responsible, either directly or indirectly, for the death of at least five other characters in the tragedy before he finally kills Claudius.[18]

[17] In *Dark Legend: A Study in Murder* (London, 1947), Frederic Wertham made a strong case, clinically as well as in literary terms, for Orestes as the Greek tragic figure who provides the closest analogy for Hamlet.

[18] Introduction to the New Penguin *Hamlet*, p. 36.

One of the means by which the play accomplishes that feat is by presenting the major conflict within Hamlet's mind and soul as a conflict between a view of human life and the universe as admirable and even blessed ('this goodly frame the earth. . . . What piece of work is a man'—II. ii. 298-303), and a view of an individual supernaturally devoted to the single-minded and private pursuit and murder of an uncle, a stepfather, and a king. It is, we recognize, literally impossible for anyone to retain the former view and choose to act in the latter fashion. If a hero attempts to do so, he will suffer astonishingly: he will likely come to view the world as corrupt and diseased rather than 'goodly'; he may experience moral and sexual nausea; he may come near to madness; and he may wish, momentarily at least, to die.

However, the primary reason that Hamlet cannot come to firm and continuous resolution to undertake the murder of Claudius probably has less to do with moral or psychological issues than with dramatic ones—it may be less a problem for Hamlet (or for Shakespeare) than for the audience. It is we who cannot bear that such a golden figure,[19] an ideal prince supremely gifted, should kill in cold blood. The conventions, both dramatic and fictional, may be morally questionable, but they are relatively clear. We can contemplate the moral decline, decay, and death of a relatively flawed figure with interest and even fascination. Thus the limited and relatively unintelligent Laertes simple-mindedly becomes the tool of Claudius, and, abandoning all values except those of revenge and betraying his own honour in the name of honour, dies by his own dishonourable weapons; and we, along with Hamlet, can forgive him when he repents, confesses, and asks pardon. We will watch with horror the spiritual suicide and eventual death of a heroic figure like Macbeth who, consumed by ambition, knowingly makes a pact with evil. We can acknowledge the fact that

---

[19] Madeleine Doran has written acutely of the unusual degree to which we identify our own humanity with Hamlet's: 'Through his responses to the false notes in the language of others Hamlet is established as the touchstone of truth. This function is dramatically important. For we see the world always through his eyes, and we must trust without question his own honesty of intent. He uses words himself in a great variety of ways, and we must feel, beneath all the exaggerations, the self-reproaches, the rages, the witty jibes and the bitter taunts, the passionate earnestness in his search for truth' (*Shakespeare's Dramatic Language*, p. 46).

inflexible heroic figures like Coriolanus or even Lear will almost inevitably be destroyed by the changing demands of the world and their own ignorance and failures in sympathy or love; we will watch the process with compelling interest as well as pain. We can accept, however regretfully, the fact that even ideal, golden heroes do not always win, but may be defeated and killed by the forces of evil and the accidents and fortunes of time and this world. What we cannot accept is that a figure who has been made supremely attractive on stage, with whom we are led to identify almost completely since he seems to anticipate and to surpass us in every way, should alienate us by both deciding and acting (upon whatever compulsion) to kill another in cold blood.[20] He can, of course, kill any number of people upon impulse, when emotionally aroused: that is an understandable response which need not sacrifice our sympathies either on stage or off. He may kill hundreds in open warfare and numbers in duels, with opponents who can defend themselves and with the conventions open and recognized. But he cannot realistically plan a secret assassination, or stab someone in the back, or poison a supposedly innocuous drink, or cheat with an unbated and poisoned sword, or lunge instead of break after a fencing referee has rendered judgement.

Hamlet can argue that he *should* plan and execute the murder, he can berate himself for moral weakness and cowardice, he can argue that it would be a sin *not* to kill Claudius—and almost convince us, since there seems to be no other way in which guilt can be discovered and punished and justice re-established in Denmark; but he cannot do it. Pushed perilously close to the madness which he so conveniently simulates, distraught by the ghost's revelations and commands, his imagination of the potentialities of human life and sexuality as poisoned as Lear's ('Let copulation thrive'), Hamlet can speak cruelly to Ophelia as a signal sharer in universal female depravity—while at the same time he tries to warn her that she must abandon all

---

[20] In *Crime and Punishment* Dostoevsky caused an intelligent and sensitive figure to plan and execute a murder without alienating the sympathies of his readers; in the event, however, the planning becomes an insane obsession, and the execution a diseased and terrifying nightmare as far as possible from cold-blooded resolution or determination. The ill Raskolnikov remains the 'hero' with whom we sympathize. Through his suffering, his punishment, and Sonia's love he can be forgiven—by his readers, by himself, and, we are led to believe, by God.

thought of him. Enormously excited by Claudius's self-betrayal after the play scene, fearful that he might even kill his mother, he can 'speak daggers' to Gertrude and, in fury, almost immediately stab through the arras what he thinks is the eavesdropping Claudius, with relief that, in the passionate moment, he believes he has accomplished his duty of revenge. He is, moreover, relatively unmoved by the sight of the dead Polonius:

> Thou wretched, rash, intruding fool, farewell.
> I took thee for thy better. Take thy fortune:
> Thou find'st to be too busy is some danger.
> (III. iv. 31-3)

In immediate fury at the discovery that Rosencrantz and Guildenstern carry secret official orders from Claudius for his own death, Hamlet can invent and dispatch the substitute orders that his treacherous friends should be executed in his stead. But he cannot coolly plan and carry out the deliberate murder of Claudius—or anyone else—at a future point in time.

If Hamlet has a flaw or weakness, it may be his very appetite for life. It is impossible to imagine a conscious Hamlet literally in a state of 'bestial oblivion'; but Hamlet accuses himself of such a state as he comes to recognize that, when not overcome with grief or melancholy and the sense that it is impossible for him to act significantly, he deeply desires to continue to live, to observe, to respond, to act, even to play, rather than to undertake a role as a calculating revenger. For him to devote himself fully to such a role, whether he conceives it as becoming the proper avenger of family honour or the superhuman scourge and minister of the state of Denmark, would inevitably involve the death of almost everything that he has loved and been.

It is only with the gravediggers' scene that Hamlet is able to accept his destiny. Those two marvellous clowns who pretentiously argue about theological and legal judgements of human actions that are quite beyond them, and contentedly sing of love and age and death as they spend their lives digging their daily graves, provide an astonishingly shifted perspective for the audience as well as Hamlet. Both Hamlet and we who have watched and heard him have been intensely and anxiously concentrating on conflicting psychological, moral, and perhaps even theological imperatives or questions which seem to require

immediate reconciliation or resolution, as well as plots, in-
trigues, and traps demanding immediate decisions and
actions. The gravediggers suddenly present us with a perspective from which death is indeed 'common'—quotidian—and
dissolution is a familiar and hardly even alarming leveller of all
heroic strivings and all earthly grandeur. That distancing perspective is, inevitably, not only on death but also on life and on
all anxious efforts to decide, to plan, and to act as if men did
shape, consciously and alone, both their lives and the ever-
widening circles of influence of their deeds. For Hamlet, the
result of the shift seems to be a release, a recapture of
something of his former 'carelessness', so that he is free to respond, spontaneously, and with sorrow to Ophelia's death and
with outrageous anger to Laertes' curses (so that he can leap
into the grave, assert his princely identity, openly struggle with
Laertes and begin to overcome him);[21] free to declare his love
for Ophelia and to parody Laertes' rant; free to find Osric
amusing, to question him, and to parody his language; free to
undertake the fencing match; free, when he recognizes Laertes'
treachery and violation of honourable exchange, to execute a
remarkable bit of sword-play in which he forces Laertes to exchange weapons and wounds the poisoner with his own rapier;
and finally, with full knowledge of Claudius's crimes and his
own death, free to turn the poisoned instruments against the
source of all the poison, to struggle with Horatio and seize the
poisoned cup, to beg that Horatio live to tell his story and
defend his name, and both to prophesy and to give his voice to
the inheritance of Fortinbras.

The combination of freedom and resolution that his shifted
perspective allows Hamlet in some ways resembles the release
and determination that T. S. Eliot's Thomas à Becket achieves
after he has finally finished with all his tempters: 'I shall no

---

[21] Laertes initiates the physical struggle with 'The devil take thy soul!' (V. i. 251).
Hamlet's response ('Thou pray'st not well. / I prithee take thy fingers from my
throat, / For though I am not splenative and rash, / Yet have I in me something
dangerous, / Which let thy wiseness fear. Hold off thy hand'—ll. 252-6) suggests that
he responds effectively physically as well as verbally. Claudius's response, 'Pluck them
asunder,' makes most sense if in this, as in every other physical struggle in which he
engages within the play, Hamlet is winning. Roland Frye remarked in conversation
that it seems unlikely that Claudius would seek to intervene if Laertes were winning:
that might have presaged the 'present death of Hamlet' in which Claudius had
perceived the only possibility of his peace.

longer act or suffer, to the sword's end.'[22] Hamlet's praise of
his own rashness ('Our indiscretion sometime serves us well /
When our deep plots do pall; and that should learn us /
There's a divinity that shapes our ends, / Rough-hew them
how we will'—V. ii. 8-11) is occasioned by his recognition that
his life recently depended upon his discovery of Claudius's plot
against him through the seeming accident of his own sleepless-
ness. His decision neither to refuse nor to postpone the fencing
match despite his premonition of disaster or death stems from
his new perspective on death and his life and also from his
acceptance of purposes beyond his will or control. Like the
speaker of Eliot's 'East Coker' who says, 'For us, there is only
the trying. The rest is not our business',[23] Hamlet determines
that he will respond as well as he can to the occasions of his life
as they arise, but he will not attempt either to seek or to forestall death or fate, and he will not attempt either to predict or to
determine the ultimate effects of his actions. He responds to
Horatio's emotional 'If your mind dislikes any thing, obey it. I
will forestall their repair hither, and say you are not fit' with

Not a whit. We defy augury. There is special providence in the fall of
a sparrow. If it be now, 'tis not to come; if it be not to come, it will be
now; if it be not now, yet it will come. The readiness is all.

(V. ii. 215-18)

While 'it' seems clearly to refer to death, the 'readiness' surely
implies full alertness to life itself—whatever may come,
including death. Human life loses its claim to heroism (and
much of its interest—for the actor as well as the viewer or con-
templator) if its chief energies are devoted to avoiding or delay-
ing the coming of death or, even more unnaturally, to pursuit
of that death which will surely come.

In recent years readers who felt sure of Hamlet's manifold
psychological and moral weakness have frequently patronized

---

[22] *The Complete Poems and Plays* (London, 1969), p. 259. In 1919 Eliot wrote an
unsatisfactory essay, 'Hamlet and His Problems', in which he accepted a romantic
reading of Hamlet as a figure with excessive emotions and an incapacity for action and
then complained that the figure made for unsatisfactory drama. But as with a number
of his bold (and sometimes cranky) early judgements, such as those of Milton's and
Shelley's poetry, the rejected figures kept reappearing in Eliot's later verse and drama,
often with implications of quite different assessments.

[23] *The Complete Poems and Plays*, p. 182.

the concluding remarks spoken after his death as indicative only of the limitations of their speakers: we should, supposedly, not expect anything particularly perceptive or enlightening from that repressed neo-Stoic, Horatio, and of course the one-track military figure, Fortinbras, could not imagine an admirable figure who was not a soldier. But such responses rarely occur to attentive members of the audience at a decent performance. In the final scenes of his tragedies, Shakespeare never felt bound by conventions of psychological realism. With the chief attention of everyone, those on stage and in the audience alike, clearly focused on the bodies of the heroic dead, the survivors who will attempt to establish a new order frequently speak beyond what we would have considered to be their natural range: their voices move towards formal, public tributes and honours—adornments for the bier or tomb—which the audience, too, may share in bestowing. Within the last lines there is rarely much room for ironies that distance the speakers' responses on stage from ours within the audience. Although modern imaginations may find flights of angels singing requiem to soldiers incongruous, I believe Shakespeare's audience would have seen nothing strange at all in that image; most members of a contemporary audience that has been allowed to glimpse the gifted and heroic Hamlet that Shakespeare created will probably also find little unsuitable in Horatio's wish. The farewell of Horatio and the tribute of Fortinbras represent differing responses to Hamlet's life and death, but I believe that one easily follows the other dramatically, and that the audience is expected to join in both.

From the first moment that they meet within the play, there has been no doubt concerning Hamlet's and Horatio's friendship:

> *Enter* HORATIO, MARCELLUS, *and* BARNARDO.
> *Horatio.* Hail to your lordship.
> *Hamlet.*   I am glad to see you well.
>   Horatio, or I do forget myself.
> *Horatio.* The same, my lord, and your poor servant ever.
> *Hamlet.* Sir, my good friend, I'll change that name
>   with you.   (I. ii. 160-3)

Before the final scene, however, it is Hamlet who expresses

most of the warmth of their relationship—to the point of some comedy when he becomes extravagant in his fervent praise for Horatio's justice, his invulnerability to suffering, and his superiority to passion. Horatio has listened to Hamlet, and he has helped him watch Claudius during the play; after the revelation of Claudius's plot to have Hamlet killed in England, Horatio finally exclaimed, 'Why, what a king is this!' (V. ii. 62). But he refused to answer Hamlet's urgent (even if rhetorical) questions:

> Does it not, think thee, stand me now upon—
> He that hath kill'd my king and whor'd my mother,
> Popp'd in between th'election and my hopes,
> Thrown out his angle for my proper life
> And with such coz'nage—is't not perfect conscience
> To quit him with this arm? And is't not to be damn'd
> To let this canker of our nature come
> In further evil?   (V. ii. 63-70)

In reply, Horatio only remarked that Hamlet would not have much time. Before the final lines of the play, he showed most warmth in his alarm at Hamlet's 'gaingiving' and his urging of Hamlet not to undertake the fencing match. His sudden emotional response to Hamlet's dying request that he live and 'Report me and my cause aright / To the unsatisfied' (V. ii. 344-5), then, surprises us. He seems almost to parody the calm and deliberate death of a Cato in his passionate, unpremeditated attempt to seize the cup and prove he is 'more an antique Roman than a Dane' (346). Like the deaths of Enobarbus and Eros (as also those of Iras and Charmian) in *Antony and Cleopatra*, Horatio's gesture is a moving tribute which, even posthumously, adds to the heroic stature of the central figure: one human being is so devoted to another that he would prefer to die rather than to live in a world bereft of the loved one's presence. After Hamlet struggles with him for the cup and prophesies concerning Fortinbras, Horatio responds to his dying words,

> Now cracks a noble heart. Good night, sweet prince,
> And flights of angels sing thee to thy rest.
>   (V. ii. 364-5)

It is doubtful that Horatio would ever have addressed the living

Hamlet as 'sweet prince': but at the moment of Hamlet's death, he remembers and witnesses to his nobility, his generosity, his 'sweetness'. Despite the reminder of Hamlet's official identity as 'prince', Horatio's emphasis is personal as he says a last good-night.

Only with the entrance of Fortinbras does Horatio speak in more general terms to identify the sight of that stage littered with bodies as the summation of all woe or wonder that could be seen. He begins to fulfil Hamlet's last request that he should tell his story:

> And let me speak to th'yet unknowing world
> How these things came about. So shall you hear
> Of carnal, bloody, and unnatural acts,
> Of accidental judgments, casual slaughters,
> Of deaths put on by cunning and forc'd cause,
> And, in this upshot, purposes mistook
> Fall'n on th'inventors' heads. All this can I
> Truly deliver.   (V. ii. 384-91)

But it is Fortinbras who provides the final public judgement, as he asserts his interest in the kingdom of Denmark and gives orders for funeral honours. From the text we have, there seems no possible way that Fortinbras could realistically have known much about Hamlet's private or public character, but in these final moments that does not matter at all: what he says points to the public acknowledgement of the noble and heroic qualities which we have come to know and the final ceremonial honours paid to them:

>   Let four captains
> Bear Hamlet like a soldier to the stage,
> For he was likely, had he been put on,
> To have prov'd most royal; and for his passage,
> The soldier's music and the rite of war
> Speak loudly for him.
> Take up the bodies. Such a sight as this
> Becomes the field, but here shows much amiss.
> Go, bid the soldiers shoot.   (V. ii. 400-8)

With our privileged knowledge of the private as well as the public Hamlet, we may feel that Hamlet has indeed been 'put on' in a sense that Fortinbras knows nothing about; the revelation of his extraordinary gifts of body, mind, and spirit have convinced us that he has earned a soldier's death and honours. We do not wish any more or other words. Here, for the first time, Shakespeare did not end a tragedy with the customary summary final couplet, but added an additional half-line: 'Go, bid the soldiers shoot.'[24] It is the formal procession as the bodies are carried off-stage and, surely, the dead march of the drums, 'the soldier's music', that help complete our sense of participation in the public recognition of heroic tragedy. Then comes the final peal of ordnance—primarily a salute to a fallen soldier and a noble prince, but also, as it works on stage and in our imaginations, a purging of the air of Denmark of all its plagues of disease and corruption and crime, and a final explosive release of the emotional, intellectual, and moral tensions that have built up in us as we have attended this long, complicated, disturbing, even gruelling play. After those closing sounds the members of the audience may not be universally calm of mind, but surely all their passion is spent. The peal of ordnance is the culminating and final occasion on which the primary experience of the play goes beyond the limits of what may be adequately expressed in ordinary language.[25]

[24] He seems to have remembered his successful practice in *Hamlet* in two of the later tragedies: *Coriolanus* ends with Aufidius's final 'Assist', and *Timon of Athens* ends with Alcibiades' half-line, 'Let our drums strike'. In each case, as in *Hamlet*, the line fragment seems to be completed by the sounds of the drums (both funereal and military) and the sight of the military processions as the stage is emptied.

[25] In a paper on '*Titus Andronicus, Hamlet*, and the Limits of Expressibility' presented to a seminar at the Huntington Library in 1980 (a fuller version will appear in *Hamlet Studies*), Charles Forker made the point as he discussed the many occasions on which *Hamlet* suggests emotions or experiences beyond the limits of full verbal expression.

IV

The Comedy of Justice:
Measure for Measure

There are probably more widely divergent responses today to *Measure for Measure* than to any other Shakespeare's plays, from utter hostility through simple bafflement to rapture about almost everything—characterizations, dramatic construction, morality, meaning, even the text. Quiller-Couch typified one style of commentary by beginning with the question, 'What is wrong with this play?'[1] To those who see nothing wrong with it, the question and much of the succeeding commentary may seem absurd.[2]

A number of strongly held convictions, only incidentally literary, may make response to the play difficult: that it is absurd for any girl to place extraordinary value on her virginity, that subterfuges or 'dark dealing' are always unethical, that all figures of authority and all manipulators are reprehensible, that society should always punish criminal intent as well as criminal behaviour, that a woman is a fool to marry a man who has once callously abandoned her, that postulant nuns should not marry, that the bed-trick (that insulting deflation of romantic love) is an abomination that could never be approved or practised by a decent person, that it is inhuman as well as

---

[1] *Measure for Measure*, ed. J. Dover Wilson and Arthur T. Quiller-Couch (Cambridge, 1922), p. xiii.

[2] I have found particularly challenging (and outrageous) Harriett Hawkins's essay on the play in her brilliant volume, *Likenesses of Truth in Elizabethan and Restoration Drama* (Oxford, 1972), which Arthur Kirsch answered in 'The Integrity of *Measure for Measure*', *Shakespeare Survey 28* (1975), pp. 89-105. Among the earlier full studies, I have learned a great deal from Mary Lascelles's *Shakespeare's 'Measure for Measure'* (London, 1953) and Robert G. Hunter's *Shakespeare and the Comedy of Forgiveness* (New York, 1965). I have found the following essays particularly illuminating: Donna B. Hamilton's 'The Duke in *Measure for Measure*: "I find an Apt Remission in Myself," ' *Shakespeare Studies*, 6 (1972), 175-83; James Black's 'The Unfolding of *Measure for Measure*', *Shakespeare Survey 26* (1973, pp. 119-28; and Lucy Owen's 'Mode and Character in *Measure for Measure*', *Shakespeare Quarterly*, 25 (1974), 17-32. Louise Schleiner's excellent 'Ethical Improvisation in *Measure for Measure*' (*PMLA* 97 (1982), 227-36) appeared after I had completed my essay.

absurd to forgive the hypocritical murderer of one's brother—the list suggests the extent to which Shakespeare's play is, among other things, a 'morality', although hardly of the medieval variety. Readers with strong convictions concerning literary genres are also likely to feel unsettled here. The play is intractable to notions of comedy as purely joyous, relatively free from disturbing anxieties and serious concerns. It disturbs, too, those who think 'potentially tragic' characters should always be given the freedom to commit and perhaps also to expiate their crimes or errors of judgement, as well as many who have precise notions about what tragicomedy should be.

A good deal of the dissatisfaction with the play has focused on the character of the Duke. Critics have seen Vincentio as lazy, devious, and irresponsible, as well as manipulating, cold, and authoritarian.[3] But if we pay close attention to the way we experience the play in the theatre, we may conclude that, if blame is due, it should be directed to a larger figure; for it is surely the playwright rather than the Duke who is responsible for most of our perplexities—particularly those deriving from the oddities of the play's construction. Most of Shakespeare's plays introduce all the major characters in the opening scenes. By the end of Act I, or, occasionally, the first scenes of Act II, we know the world of the play and the characters who inhabit it; if we are attentive, we are in a position to judge the initial situations and to anticipate likely developments.[4] In *Measure for Measure*, however, new characters appear continually and, although the presence of Duke Vincentio assures us of limits to the possibilities of catastrophe, we are unsure both of his precise aims and of his means: we cannot at all predict what will happen.[5] Scholars and critics ordinarily assume a superior,

---

[3] Patrick Swinden, *An Introduction to Shakespeare's Comedies* (London, 1973), p. 152.

[4] Rarely, an additional figure or figures may be introduced at the end, but their functions are usually incidental, celebratory, or symbolic.

[5] Act I introduces eleven named characters, two loquacious anonymous gentlemen, and a vague number of Lords and Attendants and Officers—surely enough to swell the stage sufficiently for most plays. The mysteriously laconic Justice appears in II. i along with Elbow and Froth; then in II. ii we meet the Provost and his servant. In Act III we meet only those we already know, but Mariana and her singing boy appear in IV. i and Abhorson in IV. ii. In IV. iii we see the literally irrepressible Barnardine and at least the head of Ragozine. In IV. v comes Varrius, apparently a courtier in the confidence of the Duke, who gives symbolic stage reality to those other new figures so precisely named (Valencius, Rowland, Crassus, Flavius) who are engaged with him in

'adult' point of view towards extraordinary events on stage. Our understanding provides a comfortable distancing which assures us that we will not share directly the confusions and enthusiasms of the characters we watch: we will not be help-lessly overcome—or deceived. But in this play, without either obviously supernatural interventions or proper clues for the *cognoscenti*, we are reduced to a state of childlike waiting for the revelation of wonders by a secretive Duke and a mysterious playwright. The form of the play has continually reminded us that its world, like the number of its characters, is larger than our knowledge, or anticipation, or perhaps even imagination. In its last scene it dares to present a sort of masque of Judge-ment in which we, the true judges, are defeated, as we are in-vited to be baffled by and then to rejoice in a complicated, limited, in some respects grimy and all too realistic working out of a happy ending that has suggested for numbers of viewers (either to their delight or dismay) some sort of relation with the almost unimaginable dream of the full reconciliation of justice and mercy—justice fully satisfied and yet everyone forgiven, the war in God's face resolved, Righteousness and Peace kis-sing each other—that moment beyond time when both 'sin is behovely' and 'all shall be well.'[6]

The result is that while some readers try to respond to the entire play as admirable religious allegory, others find it—or part of it—badly constructed, inconsistent, unbelievable, dis-honest, or even hateful.[7] Jonathan R. Price has argued that such passionately held contradictory opinions are paradoxical

the secret preparations for the ultimate scene of discovery; and in the same thirteen-line scene, we first meet Friar Peter. Although a number of editors assume that Friar Peter is our old acquaintance Friar Thomas, misnamed by a careless author or printer, the extraordinary way in which new characters continue to be introduced may offer dramatic point to Peter's being still another Friar. Act V introduces no new named characters, but for the first time the stage directions indicate that Citizens are present to witness, along with the audience in the theatre, the intricate disentangling of these dark events and the public judgements of justice and mercy.

[6] The phrases from Chapter 27 of Julian of Norwich's *Revelations of Divine Love* are best known today in T. S. Eliot's quotations within 'Little Gidding'.

[7] As unsympathetic readers tick off the moral failings of all the supposedly admir-able characters in the play, Isabella's question to Angelo may ring out with unusual irony: 'How would you be / If He, that is the top of judgement, should / But judge you as you are?' (II. ii. 75-7). I quote throughout from the New Arden text edited by J. W. Lever (London, 1965).

evidence of the play's success.[8] At least playgoers rarely find it boring. In fact, if one has been lucky enough to attend a performance in which everything worked, when one was startled, moved, delighted, and left the theatre both astonished and thankful, one is unable to exchange the memory of that experience for notions of strict religious allegory, a broken-backed play, a fumbling or cynical dramatist, or impossible or unsympathetic characters, however learned or intelligent the critical arguments.

I was lucky to attend a performance of Margaret Webster's production at the Old Vic in 1957.[9] But even if one has experienced the success of the play, one may be puzzled by how it is achieved. How does Shakespeare raise desperate problems of social order and personal ethics and then dare not to pretend really to solve them? How can he bring matters of death and of anguished or corrupt sexuality—transposed heads and transposed bodies—on stage along with, or closely followed by, jokes and laughter and supposed resolutions in a number of marriages? I believe that from the first lines, he attempted the most

8 'The contradictions are set up and we are encouraged to try to resolve them. We are constantly being given new and different information, and having to readjust our opinions. We lean forward trying to figure out exactly what is going on—and we are hooked' ('*Measure for Measure* and the Critics: Towards A New Approach', *Shakespeare Quarterly*, 20 (1969), 198). Price's is in many ways an attractive position: readers do become passionately engaged with the drama. However, I do not believe it likely that playgoers would become so engaged with a production that merely attempted to 'hook' them by emphasizing mutually exclusive possibilities.

9 At the time I had taught the play several times and thought I knew it well, its strengths as well as its weaknesses, the places where Shakespeare had nodded or scurried; while I recognized the power of certain scenes, I thought some scenes and lines *could* not be played effectively. Despite the fact that I did not care for John Neville's Angelo, I left the theatre convinced that *Measure for Measure* is one of Shakespeare's greatest plays, and that there should be no more essays on it—only an available film of that production. There was, so far as I know, no film. Mary Clarke gives details of the production in *Shakespeare at the Old Vic*, 5 (1957-8). Barbara Jefford triumphed as Isabella (as she had in Peter Brook's 1950 production at Stratford) and Anthony Nicholls was splendid as the Duke. The play was warmly received by the critics, and after a slow start had just begun to draw good crowds (I got the last two seats for the last Saturday matinée) when it was taken off to make way for the Christmas production of *A Midsummer Night's Dream*.

Before she undertook her production, Miss Webster had remarked in *Shakespeare Today* (London, 1957), pp. 249-50, that *Measure for Measure* is a play in which silences are unusually important (a point I had previously missed), and had asked rhetorically, 'Unless we trust Shakespeare, why do we bother to produce him?' In this production, her knowledge of the theatre, theatrical tradition, and the text triumphantly justified her trust.

extraordinary control and balance of our responses from moments of almost complete engagement with the experiences presented on the stage to moments of remarkable detachment as our perspectives shift to new and unexpected points of view.[10] Unless we (and the actors and directors) pay close attention to those shifts, we may lose the play.

The most remarkable thing about the first scene is the sense of hurry. The Duke deputes his power to Angelo and assigns some responsibilities to Escalus, but we hear neither the purpose of his departure, his destination, nor the reason for the haste; at the end of the scene Angelo and Escalus have still not read their commissions. The Duke tells Escalus that he has intentionally selected Angelo as his Deputy, but not precisely why; his speech to Angelo only hints that Angelo's new power will manifest his virtues by putting them to use. Angelo is not ordered to enforce the laws, but to administer them as he thinks best. Only later are we likely to realize that the Duke did not indicate what *kind* of 'history' Angelo's life revealed to the observer (ll. 27-9); now we simply recognize that Angelo has a fine reputation. With no time for ceremonies, the Duke is gone. If we notice Angelo's farewell to the Duke, 'The heavens give safety to your purposes!', it is probably only to wonder what those purposes might be.

Scene ii, like the second scene of *I Henry IV*, contrasts hurried ceremony with leisurely low life. Lucio, the 'Fantastic', and the 'Two other like Gentlemen' are the first of the large number of characters in the play who invite laughter at almost every appearance on stage. The group includes the clown Pompey and his employer, Mistress Overdone, a 'Bawd'; Elbow, 'a simple Constable' and a male Malaprop; Froth, 'a foolish Gentleman'; Abhorson, a comically solemn Executioner and a natural partner for Pompey; and Barnardine, 'a dissolute prisoner' who triumphantly insists that a hangover and an individual's will take precedence over both the mortal judgements of the state and the consolations of the Church. Those nine comic roles should provide difficulties for those who resist recognizing *Measure for Measure* as a comedy. Although Lucio's

[10] Here, as elsewhere, I am indebted to Maynard Mack's 'Engagement and Detachment in Shakespeare's Plays', *Essays on Shakespeare and Elizabethan Drama in Honour of Hardin Craig*, ed. Richard Hosley (Columbia, 1962), pp. 275-96.

opening remarks suggest that the Duke's haste has some secret political or military motive (as we might expect in a play that begins with the delegation of sovereign power), the conversation immediately becomes scurrilously comic as it turns to the gaps between sanctimonious language and human desires (praying for peace while longing for war, pirates reciting the Ten Commandments), accusations of life without 'grace' in any form, and insistent innuendoes of venereal disease. Mistress Overdone's announcement that one 'worth five thousand of you all' has been 'arrested and carried to prison' (56-7) occasions little anxiety: 'Nay, but I know 'tis so. I saw him arrested: saw him carried away: and which is more, within these three days his head to be chopped off' (61-3). Perhaps it is that 'chopped off' that makes it seem as unlikely to the audience as to Lucio that the report is true—particularly when associated with its supposed occasion: 'and it is for getting Madam Julietta with child' (66-7). The two gentlemen refer vaguely to former conversation and a proclamation, but it is Pompey, pimp and tapster, who states the details of Claudio's predicament and the new legal developments in a tone which makes the news almost impossible to take seriously:

Pompey. You have not heard of the proclamation, have you?
Mistress Overdone. What proclamation, man?
Pompey. All houses in the suburbs of Vienna must be plucked down.
Mistress Overdone. And what shall become of those in the city?
Pompey. They shall stand for seed: they had gone down too, but that a wise burgher put in for them. (85-92)[11]

It is only with the entrance of the procession (Provost, Officers, Claudio and Juliet, Lucio, and the two Gentlemen) that we discover matters are indeed serious: Claudio is to be displayed to the public as an offender, imprisoned, and perhaps executed. But Claudio's declamation on the abuses of liberty ('A thirsty evil; and when we drink, we die'—l. 122) is deflated by Lucio's response: 'If I could speak so wisely under an arrest, I would send for certain of my creditors; and yet, to say

---

[11] J. W. Lever (Arden edition, pp. xix-xx) argues that lines 79-85 were mistakenly printed in the Folio from copy which should have shown them excised—although Pompey may be referring to 'yonder man' off stage whom Mistress Overdone does not see. The point does not affect my argument concerning the tone of the dialogue between Pompey and Overdone, which remains consistent to line 105.

the truth, I had as lief have the foppery of freedom as the morality of imprisonment' (123-6). Lucio seems to admire Claudio's moral rhetoric so much that for a moment he can almost imagine sharing its sentiment; yet we cannot keep from laughing when his cheerfully cynical sense of reality quickly reasserts itself. Unlike Iago or Thersites or the aggressive or even tortured sexual cynics created by other Jacobean dramatists, Lucio (like Autolycus) never seriously threatens our persons or our sensibilities. His malice is relatively unfocused, he is willing to go to some trouble to help a friend, and he remains smugly cocky until the end. When he leaves the stage, a strange messenger to a sister about to enter a cloister, the tone of his lines assures us that, whatever the threats, we will laugh at this play—and we will probably end with some sort of vision of the continuance of life:

I pray she may [persuade well]: as well for the encouragement of the like, which else would stand under grievous imposition, as for the enjoying of thy life, who I would be sorry should be thus foolishly lost at a game of tick-tack.—I'll to her.   (I. ii. 177-81)

The violent or absurd contrasts of the opening scenes (Duke and Deputy followed by madam and pimp, a man condemned to death for impregnating his fiancée in a society where fornication —or at least talk of it—seems the chief activity, pseudo-tragic emotion juxtaposed with comic obscenity) truly introduce us to this play. In scene iii, our expectations of comedy—or at least of the avoidance of tragedy—are reinforced when we discover that the Duke has remained in Vienna disguised as a friar: the superior power is present which can intervene to prevent catastrophe. But the scene is almost as interesting for what it does not tell us as for what it does. It begins with the Duke assuring Friar Thomas that he is not engaged in amorous adventure— another of the expected reasons why gentlemen and rulers on stage and in romances go incognito. His initially suggested motive for his behaviour is odd: he has 'let slip' the 'strict statutes and most biting laws' for 'this fourteen years', and the result has been general social disorder. The problem does not seem to be a matter of the Duke's excessive mercy but of his negligence; like a later Shakespearian Duke, he has simply withdrawn from his duties as ruler. When the Friar remarks that 'It rested in your Grace / To unloose this tied-up justice when you pleas'd', the Duke's response (35-45) hardly puts an end to our questions concerning his motives and plans. While it would be both arbitrary and capricious for a ruler to move suddenly, without warning, from total neglect to strict enforcement of laws, surely a general announcement could prepare a people for such a change. Something else is involved, however cloudy. The fact that it is to be Angelo who will decide what kind of law enforcement is to follow the Duke's laxity, who will determine to what extent mercy may temper justice, and even choose which laws should be first enforced, implicitly suggests the question whether we (or Vienna) would prefer to live under a negligent ruler or under reformed rule by a Deputy of 'stricture and firm abstinence'.[12] The Duke assures Friar Thomas that at 'more leisure' he will give more reasons for his actions, but we never hear them; we hear only the reason most important for our response to the play:

> Lord Angelo is precise;
> Stands at a guard with Envy; scarce confesses
> That his blood flows; or that his appetite
> Is more to bread than stone. Hence shall we see
> If power change purpose, what our seemers be.
> (I. iii. 50-4)

We already know that a man who dreams of his own perfection and refuses to admit that his blood flows or that he is subject to human appetites cannot be what he seems. The interesting questions will be: what happens to the state when a self-righteous precisian is given absolute power? and, what happens to such a man's inner being and behaviour when such power provides temptations beyond his imagination or desire?

Within five lines of the Duke's description of Angelo, we discover in the succeeding scene that the novice Isabella desires a 'more strict restraint' than the order of Poor Clares provides: the analogy is unmistakable. A rule so strict that one cannot

---

[12] The vision of a disorderly world, a world turned upside down, may have been the ultimate evil for numbers of medieval and Renaissance political theorists, but it is a fairly normal condition, during moments at least, within a great many comedies. By the end of this comedy, we surely prefer such a world, with the loss of decorum and babies beating nurses, to a world right side up with a large percentage of its inhabitants condemned to death.

both speak and show one's face to a member of the opposite sex is almost unimaginable in the world of comedy. In wishing it more strict, Isabella is at this point as self-righteous as Angelo. From Lucio's opening address ('Hail virgin, if you be—as those cheek-roses / Proclaim you are no less'—I. iv. 16-17) we are rarely allowed simply to identify with her responses. Her initial exclamation at Claudio's predicament ('O, let him marry her!') is sympathetic and practical; but when Lucio assures her that Claudio will die without her intervention, Isabella shrinks from the encounter. Although the tone of the scene is predominantly serious, Lucio's language, with the sexual implications in how men 'give' to maidens who sue, and are helpless before abject femininity, makes it anything but single. There is a suggestion of a further test of how power may change purpose and reveal character.

Act II, scene i resumes the pattern of serious debates which sharpen differences conjoined with comic passages which undermine them. Angelo argues that the issues in Claudio's case are simply those of justice and anarchy while Escalus insists that there must be some alternative to the death penalty if the purpose of law is the good of society. But the mood created by Escalus's perplexity and pity[13] is shattered when Constable Elbow rushes in with those 'notorious benefactors', Froth and Pompey Bum, 'void of all profanation in the world, that good Christians ought to have' (II. i. 55-6). The episode splendidly demonstrates the paralysis of legal or other judgement before a shower of irrelevantly circumstantial evidence and a prosecution lost in linguistic confusion. Vaguely obscene suggestions dissolve attempts at justice in laughter:

Escalus. Come, you are a tedious fool. To the purpose: what was done to Elbow's wife that he hath cause to complain of? Come me to what was done to her.
Pompey. Sir, your honour cannot come to that yet.
Escalus. No, sir, nor I mean it not.
Pompey. Sir, but you shall come to it, by your honour's leave.

(115-21)

Although we never learn precisely what did happen to Elbow's

---

[13] 'Well, heaven forgive him; and forgive us all. / Some rise by sin, and some by virtue fall . . . / And some condemned for a fault alone' (II. i. 37-40).

wife,[14] Pompey's profession is clear, and Froth's habits and intentions relatively so. Angelo, however, impatiently abandons the hearing to Escalus, with the hope that he will 'find good cause to whip them all', evidently without thought of a severer sentence: the supposed legal absolutist is remarkably inconsistent.[15] It is Pompey who pronounces judgement on the result of an absolute enforcement of the law that provides the death penalty for fornication:

> If you head and hang all that offend that way but for ten year together, you'll be glad to give out a commission for more heads: if this law hold in Vienna ten year, I'll rent the fairest house in it after three pence a bay. If you live to see this come to pass, say Pompey told you so.   (235–40)

The experiment of Angelo's government seems an absurd dream from which Vienna must awake; the scene's more than two hundred lines of comic shambles help assure us that it will.[16]

Act II, scene ii is the first of the three scenes for which some readers have claimed tragic status. Here the duel between Isabella and Angelo, as advocates of justice and mercy, death and life, makes for splendid theatre, and Isabella speaks some of Shakespeare's most memorable lines of verse; but Shakespeare makes it difficult to respond to them with a single, tragic perspective. In the framing, introductory lines, the Provost's sympathetic incredulity[17] is neatly set against Angelo's determination and his gift for the chilling, dehumanizing phrase ('See you the fornicatress be remov'd'). The Provost remains on stage throughout the interview while Lucio prevents the reluctant Isabella from giving up after Angelo's first denial, instructs her how to employ 'winning graces', and encourages

[14] 'There was nothing done to her once' (II. i. 140).

[15] Perhaps it is that no unmarried pregnant woman here provides ultimate legal evidence; more likely, the social status of these characters is not sufficiently elevated to make them significant examples for the admonition of others.

[16] The ending of the scene provides one of the play's few suggestions for realistic civic reform. Since those of 'any wit' are as reluctant as the Duke had been to attend to the duties of governing, they pay the Elbows of this world to do it for them; Escalus plans to get the names of better qualified candidates for constable—and perhaps to apply some official pressure.

[17] 'Alas, / He hath but as offended in a dream; / All sects, all ages smack of this vice, and he / To die for't!' (ll. 3–6).

her as she begins to learn. The phrase 'your honour', introduced by the Provost in line 14, echoes with increasing irony[18]
until Isabella's final 'Save your honour' is completed by the
solitary Angelo: 'From thee: even from thy virtue!' The asides
of Lucio and the Provost mark both Isabella's gradual change
from coldly proper petitioner to passionate advocate of mercy
and Angelo's parallel change from 'indeed justice' to astonished
victim of lust. Lucio's language frequently suggests a latent
sexual dimension: 'Kneel down before him, hang upon his
gown; / You are too cold' (44-5); 'You are too cold' (56); 'Ay,
touch him: there's the vein' (70). After Isabella's moving
invocation of Christian atonement and the contrast between
'Merciful Heaven' and the thunder of 'proud man', Lucio
marks Angelo's moral collapse with an exclamation which
suggests obscene possibilities:

> O, to him, to him, wench! He will relent;
> He's coming: I perceive't.   (125-6)

Act II, scene iii reminds us that the disguised Duke is alert
and active. It is particularly welcome before II, iv, the only
occasion when we see two characters in a major struggle over
issues of life and death and honour without either a prefatory
comic scene or a stage audience which deflects or qualifies our
concerns. Although it is probably here that the play comes
nearest to tragedy, it is still not very near. Angelo's opening
soliloquy about his inward division and his inability to pray
somewhat resembles Claudius's famous soliloquy in *Hamlet*, but
it is startlingly distanced by the traditional comic actor's direct
assurance to the audience that his confession or action is secret:
Angelo's 'yea, my gravity, / Wherein—let no man hear me—
I take pride' is close in effect to Falstaff's 'No man sees me'
when he stabs Hotspur. And Angelo's confession has as much
in common with Malvolio's as with Claudius's: he has worked
hard to study 'state' (conned it by great swarths?), and he has
deliberately cultivated his rigid notions of propriety; now, he
would happily change his gravity for a plume—or perhaps
cross-gartered stockings:

> The state whereon I studied
> Is, like a good thing being often read,

[18] In lines 25, 27, 28, 42, 158.

> Grown sere and tedious; yea, my gravity,
> Wherein—let no man hear me—I take pride,
> Could I with boot change for an idle plume
> Which the air beats for vain.   (7-12)

In context, even lines such as 'Heaven in my mouth, / As if I did but only chew his name, / And in my heart the strong and swelling evil / Of my conception' (4-7), 'Blood, thou art blood', and the reference to the devil's horn[19] may suggest tragic dilemma less than the comic dismay before tumescence of a man who has always believed that his will and reason controlled his life.

When the servant announces, 'One Isabel, a sister, desires access to you', Angelo's reply, 'Teach her the way', suggests both a sexual quibble and the major question of the next hundred lines: can this man of state and public justice find, or bring himself to utter, a language which will make his desires and purposes clear to the innocent Isabella? Although Angelo has acknowledged that blood is blood, he is still shocked at the way it behaves.[20] His quibbling response to Isabella's initial 'I am come to know your pleasure' is comically predictable: 'That you might know it, would much better please me, / Than to demand what 'tis' (32-3). Angelo oddly argues that one might as well pardon a murderer as an unlawful father because it is as *easy* to kill as to impregnate. He tries to move indirectly towards his goal by means of a theoretical problem presented in chillingly mechanical terms: what *if*

> there were
> No earthly mean to save him, but that either
> You must lay down the treasures of your body
> To this suppos'd, or else to let him suffer:
> What would you do?   (94-8)

---

[19] Lines 15-17; see William Leigh Godshalk, ' "The Devil's Horn": Appearance and Reality', *Shakespeare Quarterly*, 23 (1972), 202-5.

[20] 'O heavens, / Why does my blood thus muster to my heart, / Making both it unable for itself / And dispossessing all my other parts / Of necessary fitness?' (ll. 19-23). Angelo compares his blood's behaviour to that of the 'foolish throngs' who crowd around one who faints and to the *hoi polloi* who rush to a king, 'Quit their own part, / and in obsequious fondness / Crowd to his presence, where their untaught love / Must needs appear offence' (ll. 28-30). The possibility of an allusion to King James's dislike of crowds is less important here than Angelo's notion that his blood is unmannerly to threaten his sense of noble selfhood.

The tone resembles the bloodless one of our casuists of situational ethics and advocates of 'triage'—as if it were proper, even mature, to spend our time rationally calculating intolerable and dehumanizing choices instead of praying to be delivered from them. Isabella could never entertain such a monstrous bargain. Quite apart from her supposed personality or even her status as a postulant, she can perceive moral sophistry: 'Ignomy in ransom and free pardon / Are of two houses: lawful mercy / Is nothing kin to foul redemption' (111-13).[21]

By line 120, Angelo seems to be defeated. Isabella has fully rejected his theoretical proposition, and he cannot bring himself to speak openly. But after his uncharacteristic admission, 'We are all frail', and Isabella's agreement, he resolves to 'be bold'. He urges Isabella to put on 'the destin'd livery' of frailty (he seems to consider it more properly the livery of women than of men) and at last declares openly, 'Plainly conceive, I love you' (140). This is as close to expressing tenderness or emotional commitment as Angelo ever comes; immediately afterwards, when he assures her that Claudio will not die 'if you give me love', he reduces 'love' to a single act of intercourse under threat of a loved one's death. When Angelo forgetfully swears 'on mine honour', Isabella is not only astounded and outraged,[22] but also, it seems, immensely relieved. Released

---

[21] Some readers have taken seriously Angelo's argument that agreeing to the bargain would not be a serious sin: 'I talk not of your soul: our compell'd sins / Stand more for number than for accompt' (ll. 57-8). Samson's response to the Chorus's suggestion in *Samson Agonistes* that 'Where the heart joins not outward acts defile not' comes nearer to expressing the heroic judgement which Isabella assumes here:

Where outward force constrains, the sentence holds;
But who compels me to the temple of Dagon,
Not dragging? the Philistian lords command.
Commands are no constraints. If I obey them,
I do it freely; venturing to displease
God for the fear of man, and man prefer,
Set God behind; which in his jealousy
Shall never, unrepented, find forgiveness.
(ll. 1368-76)

(I quote from the text of Douglas Bush, *The Complete Poetical Works*, Boston, 1965.) The 'bargain' is, of course, purely theoretical. Angelo discovers that he cannot let Claudio live, since he comes to believe that a living Claudio would avenge his and his sister's honour. Had Isabella agreed, she would have had no recourse within the play except penance (in the nunnery?) or death—neither reconcilable with comedy.

[22] Once again we hear the interrogative 'Ha?'. Angelo used it in II. ii. 164: 'who sins most, ha?' All seven occurrences of 'ha' in this play are predominantly interrogative, in contrast to the exclamatory 'ha's' of *King Lear*.

from her former painful moral casuistry, she now assumes that
her new knowledge of Angelo has provided her power sufficient
in itself to save Claudio. In the coldness and absolute confidence of Angelo's reply, we experience fully a recognition that
comedy sometimes works hard to prevent: that ordinary innocent citizens have in the normal course of things no protection
at all against the workings of disguised and powerful evil in
high places:

> Who will believe thee, Isabel?
>
> . . .
>
>   I have begun,
> And now I give my sensual race the rein:
> Fit thy consent to my sharp appetite;
> Lay by all nicety and prolixious blushes
> That banish what they sue for. Redeem thy brother
> By yielding up thy body to my will;
> Or else he must not only die the death,
> But thy unkindness shall his death draw out
> To ling'ring sufferance.   (153-66)

Angelo's conscious and open evil is remarkably near that of
nineteenth-century melodramatic villains. With his bland
assumption that Isabella's blushes indicate she wants what she
pretends to reject (what woman could resist so passionate and
attractive a lover?) and the clinical precision of 'sharp appetite'
and 'yielding up thy body to my will', this man deserves to
have the bed-trick played on him if anyone ever did; perhaps
only after such a trick (with his lustful imagination and his pretensions to villainy as thoroughly humbled as his sanctimonious
image and pretensions to authority) could we find him forgivable.

We have come a long way from laughter here; Isabella's final
soliloquy returns us to comic possibilities. Her initial question,
'To whom should I complain?' expresses directly her sense of
helpless vulnerability, but the second, 'Did I tell this, / Who
would believe me?' suggests that it is almost as difficult for us
to believe what we have just seen and heard on stage as it
would be for any civil authority to believe her account of
it. The lines come close to the sort of dramatic self-conscious-
ness, an almost teasing suspension of the dramatic illusion,
that we find in Fabian's remark about the behaviour of the

cross-gartered Malvolio: 'If this were played upon a stage now, I could condemn it as an improbable fiction' (*Twelfth Night*, III. iv. 128-9). That momentary shift of focus is important for what follows. Isabella's situation is intolerable, but the way in which she formulates her resolution leaves us more rather than less detached from her suffering:

> Then, Isabel live chaste, and brother, die:
> More than our brother is our chastity.
> I'll tell him yet of Angelo's request,
> And fit his mind to death, for his soul's rest.
>
> (183-6)

Such gnomic clarity as to the relative value of a brother and one's chastity and such assurance of another's willingness to sacrifice his life deserve further testing. Melodramatic distress and heroic resolution alike are here destined for comic reduction.

Claudio, momentarily reconciled to death by the Duke-Friar's oddly cheerful version of a stoic consolation,[23] quickly loses his resolution after Isabella's entrance. Although there may be a few moments of some lightness or even laughter,[24] the exchange that follows is so painful that it would irreparably tear apart the comic fabric of the play if we were not aware that the Duke also listens and responds; when it becomes intoler-

[23] The imaginative *memento mori*, an exercise in detachment from the vanity of human wishes, was conventionally thought to be of particular moral value to those in the pride of life. The audience is, of course, assured that the Duke will not allow an execution to take place for Claudio's 'crime'. (An important reason why Shakespeare changed the crime from the impetuous rape in the sources to the impregnation of a fiancée may have been to prevent anyone possibly considering a death sentence either just or to be allowed by a good ruler.) The Duke runs through the old arguments: the evanescence of breath, the ignobleness of life, the inevitability of death, the comforts of sleep, human dissatisfaction and fickleness, the burden of riches—even the ultimate argument that the young lack riches for full enjoyment and the aged acquire the riches only as they lose the capacities. Some lines would seem cruelly harsh if addressed to an older man ('Friends hast thou none; / For thine own bowels which do call thee sire, / The mere effusion of thy proper loins, / Do curse the gout, serpigo, and the rheum / For ending thee no sooner'—II. i. 28-32)—but Claudio is young. His reply indicates that he has responded to the Duke's tone appreciatively: 'I humbly thank you. / To sue to live, I find I seek to die, / And seeking death, find life. Let it come on' (ll. 41-3). He will not desperately cling to a life which he thinks he must lose immediately.

[24] There is frequently some tense laughter in the theatre when, after Isabella's 'O, were it but my life, / I'd throw it down for your deliverance / As frankly as a pin', Claudio responds with, 'Thanks, dear Isabel' (III. i. 103-5).

able, he intervenes. His intervention and the sudden lowering of temperature from passionate verse to the cool prose of explanation and intrigue have outraged some critics, but both are necessary if the play is to fulfil the unwritten contract it has offered its viewer in the first scenes and continually renewed thereafter. The immediate result is the movement towards reconciliation of the brother and sister who have just said shameful and almost unforgivable things to each other. With the Duke's story of how Angelo abandoned Mariana we learn a new reason why he may have thought desirable a public test and revelation of Angelo's use of power. The Duke remarks of his plan, 'by this is your brother saved, your honour untainted, the poor Mariana advantaged, and the corrupt deputy scaled' (253-6). Isabella, who had earlier sworn she would not even bend down to prevent Claudio's death, undertakes with some enthusiasm the plan to substitute Mariana for herself in Angelo's garden house: 'The image of it gives me content already' (260). The chief difference between Isabella's and Mariana's undertaking the sexual encounter with Angelo is surely less a matter of legal or ecclesiastical technicalities than of the simple fact that Isabella, with good reason, loathes him while Mariana, however irrationally, still loves him and wishes to be his wife.

Although the play presents intrigue as the sole means to avoid death and dishonour without the overt intervention of supreme authority, it does not allow us to accept the plan as contentedly as Isabella does: immediately after her exit Elbow enters, with the Officers and the arrested Pompey, muttering, 'Nay, if there be no remedy for it, but that you will needs buy and sell men and women like beasts, we shall have all the world drink brown and white bastard' (III. ii. 1-4), and the Duke exclaims, 'O heavens, what stuff is here!' Just after a ruler plans, for moral reasons, to substitute one woman for another in a secret midnight tryst, he is confronted with a prisoner arrested for pimping. His discomfort anticipates his comic vulnerability before Lucio's charge that before the absent Duke 'would have hanged a man for the getting a hundred bastards, he would have paid for the nursing a thousand', not simply out of charity but because 'He had some feeling of the sport' (113-17). Once the Duke moves to intervene as something of a secular providence attempting to provide a happy ending, he becomes the partial object of our laughter rather than the ceremonious director of it.

Like the playwright, he thinks he knows the characters with whom he is dealing, but he finds that they can surprise him and require awkward interventions or sudden improvisations when they seem determined to turn his comedy into a tragedy. Like God, according to Milton's conception at least, he has restricted his absolute freedom by allowing individuals also to possess significant freedom. With evil both powerful and disguised, he must intervene if his subjects are not to destroy each other and themselves, and his intervention may expose him to suffering and ridicule. But his temporary suspensions of their freedom are calculated to return individuals to themselves, with new beginnings and new freedom. On few occasions, however, was Shakespeare more insistent on the distance between the ways of the ordinary world and those of heaven than in his presentation of the Vienna of *Measure for Measure*. Although most citizens, off stage as well as on, could surely expect a little more foresight from their rulers than they actually receive, any mortal, duke or king or whatever, who seriously undertakes to imitate the power of divine providence is surely lucky if his efforts only make him appear occasionally absurd or comic rather than terrifying and insane.

One can sympathize with the Duke's disgust at the notion of life as a bawd ('Canst thou believe thy living is a life, / So stinkingly depending?'—III. ii. 25-6), but it ignores Pompey's subversive observation, ''Twas never merry world since, of two usuries, the merriest was put down, and the worser allowed by order of law; a furred gown to keep him warm; and furred with fox on lambskins too, to signify that craft, being richer than innocency, stands for the facing' (6-10).[25] Although no one has any illusions about Pompey's moral or social status,[26] and 'correction and instruction' have no salutary effect whatso-

[25] A strong case could still be made that receiving money for bringing men and women together sexually is less unnatural than the usurer's practice of causing money to 'breed' more money without the addition of fruitful labour. A few years later, Jonson made brilliant dramatic use of the traditional association of usury with perversion in *Volpone*.

[26] The Provost remarks of the relative 'weight' of Pompey and Abhorson, 'a feather will turn the scale' (IV. ii. 28-9).

ever on him, he and the other morally unregenerate characters in this play (Lucio, Barnardine, Abhorson, even Mistress Overdone) frequently display such wit or energy or dogged determination to survive that we laugh with as well as at them and welcome their appearances, however distasteful we might find them off stage. They seem to promise the defeat of any attempt at total social reformation (particularly in that area least accessible to social control, the sexual), and to threaten the dignity of would-be reformers. But our laughter is sometimes checked, or at least counterpointed, by moments of alienation—all those jocular references to syphilis, the news that Lucio had promised Kate Keep-down marriage before he had abandoned her and that he had informed against Mistress Overdone who had kept his bastard child, the Provost's reference to Barnardine as a murderer, even Pompey's comic catalogue of his imprisoned former patrons now ruined by fashion, dissipation, debt, brawls, and whoring. Anthony Caputi suggested that the scenes fluctuate between emphasis on the forces of 'civilization' and those of 'nature';[27] although the claims for each are often presented as if they were exclusive or even absolute, most of the time within the play we cannot clearly choose either, for we want the best of both and we find aspects of each intolerable or absurd. At the moments when the choices begin to seem relatively clear, some extravagance or excess or problem disturbs our perilous equilibrium, and we are engaged in new dilemmas as we are drawn deeper into the play.

Comic moments continually intrude into solemn contexts, as alienating ones (whether idealizing or gruesome) into the comic. In the first scene of Act IV, the serious tone of Isabella's relation to the Duke of her meeting with Angelo is broken by her assurance that Mariana will have no difficulty in finding the way to her tryst: 'With whispering and most guilty diligence, / In action all of precept, he did show me / The way twice o'er' (39-41). Angelo's eager diligence is close to farce. The Duke's apostrophe while Isabella tells Mariana of his plan may be a patch, but lines 60-5 are hardly irrelevant in their context.[28] Remembering his encounter with Elbow, Pompey, and Lucio

27 'Scenic Design in *Measure for Measure*', *Journal of English and Germanic Philology*, 60 (1961), 423-34.
28 Lever, Arden edition, p. 99.

just after he initiated his scheme, we recognize that he has even more cause now to feel vulnerable to 'report' and 'fancies'. The Duke's assurance, 'Come, let us go; / Our corn's to reap, for yet our tithe's to sow', is followed immediately by the Provost's and Pompey's discussion of cutting off the heads of men and women and by the humour of Abhorson. At the end of IV. ii, the Duke tries to reassure the reluctant Provost concerning his newly improvised plan to execute Barnardine early and substitute his head for Claudio's:

> Put not yourself into amazement how these things should be; all difficulties are but easy when they are known. Call your executioner, and off with Barnardine's head. I will give him a present shrift, and advise him for a better place. Yet you are amazed; but this shall absolutely resolve you. Come away; it is almost clear dawn.   (203-9)

Whether the Provost finds much comfort in such an assurance or not, most members of the audience surely feel decided uneasiness at the prospect of a happy ending procured by a hurried execution.

Those misgivings are both reinforced and put to comic use when we meet a Barnardine who strongly objects to loud noises when he has a hangover and who declines to be executed for anyone's convenience. Here is the man who truly regards death as a sleep—a drunken one: 'careless, reckless, and fearless of what's past, present, or to come: insensible of mortality, and desperately mortal' (IV. ii. 141-3). We could not have anticipated either his self-possession or the comic helplessness in which his refusal to co-operate with the usual ceremonies of state and Church would leave the official representatives of authority (IV. iii. 49-62). Of the number of occasions when the Duke's anticipations prove incorrect and his plans require hasty improvisation, this is surely the most memorable. The scene suggests how official roles and ceremonies ordinarily shelter powerful rulers and judges from experience of the human consequences of their judgements. We infer that many of them (or at least those we like best) might have considerable difficulty if they had to see and deal directly with those whom they condemn under the shelter of abstract laws and courtroom procedures.

When the Duke and the play seem to have reached an impasse, the Provost suddenly recalls that a prisoner we have never heard of before has this morning died of a fever. The Duke's response, 'O, 'tis an accident that heaven provides', nearly always occasions laughter in the theatre—an ironic recognition of the comic patness of the discovery. No character we have met is to die within this play. But when the Provost enters carrying the head of Ragozine, there are gasps from the audience: the violation of the body of even an unknown criminal who has died of natural causes may shock onlookers, particularly within a comedy. That head may suggest the physical particularity of those substituted bodies which, fortunately, we have not had to witness, as well as more general unsavoury political necessities: the shifts and stratagems to which anyone in authority may have to resort to keep the wheels turning and to prevent catastrophe.

I doubt that Shakespeare expected anyone to be satisfied with the Duke's initial explanation of why he will let Isabella think that her brother has been executed: we are puzzled—and we will learn more hereafter. The Duke offers her the chance to play a role in another dramatic performance, this time not to save her brother and her honour but to avenge them, and she agrees. We are distracted both from Isabella's grief and the Duke's brief comfort by the immediate appearance of Lucio: he plans to dine only on water and bran for fear an ampler diet might make him the next victim of the law.

The flurry of brief scenes at the end of Act IV indicate elaborate and mysterious preparations for the grand judgement scene of Act V. Most of the characters do not understand fully either what the Duke plans or the relevance of their own roles. Angelo, stricken by guilt, assumes that Isabella's 'tender shame' will prevent her from charging him with his supposed crimes, and he plans to stick to his 'seeming', officially and morally. Unknown characters are busy, and we learn from the Duke that the Provost now 'knows our purpose and our plot' and that Varrius and Friar Peter have major roles. As everyone rushes to the place before the city gates, we hear that the trumpets have sounded twice and the Duke is about to enter.[29]

[29] Act V clearly separates those who like the play as a whole from those who do not. Responses vary from those like Anne Barton (*The Riverside Shakespeare*, Boston, 1974, pp. 545, 547), who assume that almost everyone finds the last scene unsatisfactory or

Act V begins with the first noble procession of the play and
the open return and ceremonial greetings of the sovereign. The
Duke's earlier promise to Isabella and the heavy irony of his
reference to Angelo's 'desert' convince us that this is the scene
in which the hidden shall be made manifest, wrongs avenged or
resolved; yet the entire tenor of the play has assured us that,
since death and sexual violation have been prevented to the
accompaniment of frequent laughter, the judgement will not
bar forgiveness, reconciliation, and new beginnings. But no
more than the characters on stage (perhaps less than the Provost) do we know how this is to be brought about.

The word 'justice' echoes insistently and ironically. The
Duke's initial tactic seems a test of the fully ceremonial processes
of ordinary public justice: what *if* he had been truly absent
from Vienna, as all the major characters believe? Could he
through the ordinary workings of legal procedures and his own
trusted officers uncover the truth and arrive at a just judgement? The answer is a resounding, if comic, no. Without
extraordinary aid, ordinary courts, even when presided over by
men as honest as Escalus, can frequently determine little more
than affronts to conventional protocol, or to their own dignity.

We can only guess at the details of the Duke's original plans
for his display of judgement, but they could hardly have included
either his condemnation by Escalus or his subsequent discovery
by the irrepressible Lucio. We can, however, perceive his
general direction before his scenario is interrupted and he must
again improvise. From the moment of his reply to Isabella's
initial appeal, the Duke attempts to make Angelo judge his own
actions. We know Isabella's account and charges contain major
untruths, but they relate precisely what Angelo thinks is true,
and they give him the opportunity to confess to what he thinks
he has done. Except for a brief suggestion that Isabella is mad
(ll. 35-7), however, Angelo responds neither to the Duke's invitation that he should give her justice nor to her charges: he
remains silent from line 37 to line 139, while the Duke and Isa-

'notoriously troublesome' to those like Kenneth Muir ('Fifty Years of Shakespeare
Criticism: 1900-1950', *Shakespeare Survey 4* (1950), p. 14), who find it 'almost too
wonderful', arguably 'one of the most moving scenes in the canon'. Sometimes it is
oddly condemned as a theatrical 'tour de force'—as if that were clearly a pejorative
for a work written for performance in the theatre.

bella and the outrageous Lucio state or probe or elaborate the supposed revelations. The pressures on that silent figure reach a climax when the Duke scornfully demonstrates the improbability of Isabella's charges, and she is moved to a cry for patience that anticipates Lear's. But Angelo's fears that Isabella's charges may be believed are allayed. He thinks the truth has been revealed and dismissed. He has refused to confess and he seems safe.

The strange Friar Peter, however, then mysteriously announces that Isabella has 'wrongfully accused' Angelo and that he can prove her accusations false.[30] Angelo still remains silent when the veiled Mariana enters,[31] and intervenes only when she says Isabella has accused her 'husband' of fornication at the very time 'When I'll depose I had him in mine arms / With all th'effect of love' (197-8). When Mariana unveils, accuses Angelo of breaking their 'vow'd contract', and gives circumstantial details of their tryst, Angelo, again insistent on his righteousness and able to swear, with no sense of strain, upon his 'faith and honour', denies the betrothal and claims he broke off talk of marriage 'in chief / For that her reputation was disvalu'd / In levity' (219-21). He is able to recover his old self so readily partly because he is so sure of his innocence of Mariana's charge that he has almost forgotten the now seemingly discredited charges of which he was sure he was guilty. Few men would be easily convinced that their passions and senses could be so disconcertingly deceived by darkness and their imaginations. When Mariana persists with a sacred oath, kneeling in that posture of obeisance and petition which will provide the climax of the scene and the play, Angelo moves to the attack. His relief and release recall Isabella's response in II. iv. 148 ff., when, at last understanding Angelo's intentions, she also felt freed of painful theoretical concerns and able to

---

[30] The development must baffle Angelo (how can he be aided by an unknown witness who can 'prove' that what he feels sure happened did not happen?), but the Duke appeals to his sense of security and once again invites him to serve as judge.

[31] When Mariana announces that she will not remove her veil until her husband bids her, and also mysteriously admits that she is not married but is neither maid nor widow, Lucio remarks, 'My lord, she may be a punk; for many of them are neither maid, widow, nor wife!' (ll. 180-1). As Mariana continues her gnomic conundrums ('I have known my husband, yet my husband / Knew not that ever he knew me'— ll. 187-8), Lucio deflates them comically: 'He was drunk then, my lord; it can be no better' (l. 189).

act. It is refreshing to forget one's sense of guilt by concentrating on the secret plots or conspiracies of one's enemies. Pre-
tending even greater confidence in Angelo, the Duke renews
the initial experiment: Angelo shall, with the aid of Escalus,
have complete power to discover the guilty and to determine
punishments. But after asking for the 'scope of justice', Angelo
takes little part in the procedures which follow. He has never
spoken to Lucio within the course of the play; despite all of
Lucio's coaching asides to Isabella in II. ii, Angelo never
acknowledged the existence of this man who represents all that
he once despised and, after that first meeting with Isabella,
much of what he envied. The initial exchanges here between
Escalus and Lucio and the entrance of Isabella put an end to
the eagerness for judgement that Angelo felt when he faced
only Mariana:

Escalus. Pray you, my lord, give me leave to question; you shall see
how I'll handle her.
Lucio. Not better than he, by her own report.
Escalus. Say you?
Lucio. Marry, sir, I think if you handled her privately she would
sooner confess; perchance publicly she'll be ashamed.
Enter [at several doors] PROVOST *with* DUKE *[in disguise and hooded], and*
ISABELLA *[under guard].*
Escalus. I will go darkly to work with her.
Lucio. That's the way; for women are light at midnight.   (270-8)

Angelo cannot take part in that conversation. The incident
about which these men joke so casually now threatens him with
the loss of everything. He resumes silence.

'Friar Lodowick's' passionate exclamation, when he 'discovers' that the Duke has appointed Angelo as judge, is the
voice of one with an allegiance to a higher justice and authority
than Vienna's;[32] it brings out clearly that, however admirable
as a spiritual exercise for the individual, to let a man be judge
'in his own case' is intolerably unjust in legal proceedings. The
silent Angelo finds his voice only after the Duke's denunciation
of Vienna's corruption and legal disorder and Escalus's response of 'Slander to th' state! / Away with him to prison!'
(320-1): here at last is a clear and present danger to the state

---

[32] It is, however, psychologically somewhat mysterious for the Duke.

only incidentally related to his own crime. He speaks to Lucio for the first time to ask if he can provide further evidence against this treasonous man. When the Duke declares (to the audience's delight), 'I protest, I love the Duke as I love myself', Angelo exclaims at the Duke's hypocrisy; and it is Angelo who precipitates the major action when he orders Lucio to help the Provost subdue the resisting friar.

With the second discovery of a hooded or veiled figure in the scene, a new 'play' begins in which everyone finally must ask or grant pardon. With his comic response to Lucio, 'Thou art the first knave that e'er mad'st a duke', Vincentio takes open charge of justice in Vienna. Until this point Angelo has avoided or resisted all the opportunities and pressures to confess and to judge himself; he had privately regretted his action, but the thought of the knowledge and disapproval of 'power divine' did not cause him to confess until he had no choice. Now his collapse is total; the only 'grace' he seeks is the special favour of immediate death. This man who has worked so hard to develop and preserve an image of rectitude and propriety above the common lot prefers death to the humiliation of having to live with public knowledge of his frailty, corruption, and fall from power. Immediate death, he thinks, would be least painful as well as most 'just' for a man who conceived his destiny as either angelic or tragic.

Although Angelo has finally given a judgement of his own case consistent with his principles as well as his desires, the superior judicial power is now the Duke's. He first makes Angelo admit that he *was* contracted to Mariana and orders their instant marriage. When he announces his judgement for Angelo's death ('An Angelo for Claudio; death for death. / Haste still pays haste, and leisure answers leisure; / Like doth quit like, and Measure still for Measure'—407-9), he has already embarked on his last and climactic test: to make Isabella, the other representative of the highest conscious rectitude, also judge her own case. The Duke's condemnation of Angelo 'to the very block / Where Claudio stoop'd to death' sounds like the voice of ultimate judgement to most of the characters on stage; to the audience who know that the block does not exist, it provides welcome reassurance that the play will fulfil its comic promises. But the audience must also recognize the risk the Duke is taking: he cannot be sure that the girl who had wished to scratch out Angelo's eyes and had pleaded so insistently for 'justice' will refuse both apparent justice and revenge when they are offered. As the Duke turns to Lucio, Angelo's case apparently closed, the kneeling Mariana appeals to Isabella as well as the Duke:

> O my good lord—sweet Isabel, take my part;
> Lend me your knees, and all my life to come
> I'll lend you all my life to do you service.
> *Duke.* Against all sense you do importune her.
> Should she kneel down in mercy of this fact,
> Her brother's ghost his paved bed would break,
> And take her hence in horror.
> *Mariana.*   Isabel!
> Sweet Isabel, do yet but kneel by me;
> Hold up your hands, say nothing: I'll speak all.
> They say best men are moulded out of faults,
> And, for the most, become much more the better
> For being a little bad. So may my husband.
> O Isabel! Will you not lend a knee?
> *Duke.* He dies for Claudio's death.   (428-41)

It is one of the longest moments of intense suspense in Shakespeare's theatre. The claims of justice to the dead are directly opposed to those of mercy to the living. When Isabella finally kneels, she has clearly chosen mercy and life.[33]

When the Provost returns to the stage with Barnardine, Juliet, and the muffled Claudio, the final revelations and judgements are at hand. The Duke first pardons the now silent Barnardine's 'earthly faults' and prays him to 'take this mercy to provide / For better times to come' (481-3).[34] The Provost

---

[33] She has not, however, abandoned all notions of justice. Despite the dissatisfaction of Dr Johnson and many others, Isabella makes a legal point. She does not argue that Angelo should be given no punishment for his abuse of office, only against the pronounced judgement by means of an 'as if' which we know to be true: 'Most bounteous sir; / Look, if it please you, on this man condemn'd / As if my brother liv'd' (441-3). Her chief point is that, however unjust the law and harsh the punishment, Claudio was guilty of the crime with which he was charged; Angelo was not guilty of the crime with which Isabella originally charged him—he only tried to be. In kneeling, Isabella has abandoned her attempt for personal vengeance—or justice; but she tries to formulate her plea to the Duke in legal rather than religious or personal terms.

[34] Friar Peter is left with an unconscionably heavy burden: the moral admonition of Barnardine. One wonders how many more than the nine years of imprisonment he has served would be considered just in Barnardine's case by those who object to the Duke's 'unprincipled' leniency.

riddlingly answers the Duke's question, 'What muffl'd fellow's that?' while he performs the slow unmuffling of Claudio which will truly answer it. The immediate response to this third un-masking is a general moment of silent astonishment, followed by Isabella's rushing to Claudio's arms in an embrace more moving[35] than any formal speeches of reconciliation and joy that one could imagine.

The Duke's lines that immediately follow have caused a good deal of difficulty.[36] I have found no edition which prints them clearly in the way that Margaret Webster's Duke spoke them, the way that makes the most complete sense:

> [*To Isabella.*] If he be like your brother, for his sake
>   Is he pardon'd; and for your lovely sake—
> [*To Claudio.*] Give me your hand and say you will be mine—
> [*To Isabella.*] He is my brother too. But fitter time
>   for that.

According to this reading, the Duke does not 'ask for' Isabella's hand here; he only almost slips into a declaration which should be saved for a later and more private occasion. He comes near to apologizing for the warmth of 'for your lovely sake' by his insistence that he is Claudio's brother.

The Duke's 'apt remission' extends to all, apparently, except Lucio, whom he condemns to marriage, whipping, and hang-ing; but when Lucio protests only against the marriage (with its possibility of cuckoldry, the lecher's greatest fear), the comic tone is restored. The Duke forgives the slanders and therefore 'remits' the whipping and hanging, but insists that Lucio marry the mother of his child: Lucio's continued complaint, 'Marrying a punk, my lord, is pressing to death, / Whipping, and hanging' (520-1), provides the last laugh of the play.

---

[35] *The John Philip Kemble Promptbooks*, ed. Charles H. Shattuck, 6 (Charlottesville, 1974), 67, indicate that the tradition for playing the scene in this fashion is an old one.

[36] The Folio's pointing, with no stops after the second lines and only a comma after the third, is unsatisfactory both syntactically and dramatically:

> If he be like your brother, for his sake
> Is he pardon'd, and for your louelie sake
> Give me your hand, and say you will be mine,
> He is my brother too: But fitter time for that:

Most editors have experimented with the punctuation. William Allen Neilson recog-nized that the third line seems syntactically incoherent and in his edition of 1942, sensibly set it off by dashes. A number of later editors have followed his practice.

In his concluding lines, the Duke gives advice, congratulations, or thanks to each of the nuptial couples and to the Provost. There must be an extended pause in the middle of line 531, as he turns from Angelo to Isabella:

> Forgive him, Angelo, that brought you home
> The head of Ragozine for Claudio's:
> Th'offence pardons itself. Dear Isabel,
> I have a motion much imports your good;
> Whereto if you'll a willing ear incline,
> What's mine is yours, and what is yours is mine.
> So bring us to our palace, where we'll show
> What's yet behind that's meet you all should know.
>
> (529-36)

Isabella says nothing: what could she say? The secrets have been discovered, the apparent crimes 'justly' defeated by apparent punishments, and we are free to assume for all, including the noble and now wiser woman, general release and the promise of marriage.

The traditional ending of this sort of comedy is not the establishment of a well-run society with all major individual and social problems solved, not a blueprint for Utopia with the guarantee that past evils will be averted in the future (although one is usually given reason to expect that the governors will at least temporarily give additional attention to their duties), but a betrothal or a wedding feast, a beginning from which death is, for the moment, excluded. It is the occasion when it is ordinary and natural for friendly guests to wish that the lovers may live happily ever after, with hardly a thought of how miraculous the fulfilment of such a wish in this world would be. One of the oddities of *Measure for Measure* is the extent to which it insists on the perilousness of such conventions and the fragility of such moments. In that respect the viewer can be forgiven if he perceives within the play an oddly earthy and comic reflection of a dream of another happiness in another world.

V
'Look there, look there!':
The Ending of *King Lear*

A. C. Bradley suggested that, rather than emphasizing 'those sufferings [in *King Lear*] which make us doubt whether life were not simply evil, and men like the flies which wanton boys torture for their sport', 'should we not be at least as near the truth if we called the poem *The Redemption of King Lear?*'[1] and he remarked that Lear dies overcome by joy at his belief that Cordelia is alive. If Barbara Everett was correct in 1960 when she wrote that Bradley's interpretation of Lear's death 'is now accepted almost universally',[2] she was not correct for long. Hers was among the first of a rash of essays which took a firmly anti-Bradleyan stance. She concluded, 'there is little evidence in Lear's last lines for anything but his supreme tragic horror at the corpse of what had been intensely alive';[3] and in the same year J. K. Walton argued that Lear must know the 'truth' of Cordelia's death: 'There is in fact nothing in his speech . . . which indicates a transition from grief to joy.'[4] Some years later Carol Marks made the point even more emphatically: 'he dies in broken-hearted knowledge that she has "no breath at all." . . . What Lear sees is the finality of Cordelia's death, which takes from him his last motive for living.'[5] In a recent collection of essays on the play, W. F. Blissett argues that 'Look there,

[1] *Shakespearean Tragedy: Lectures on Hamlet, Othello, King Lear, Macbeth* (London, 1904), p. 245.

[2] 'The New *King Lear*', *Critical Quarterly*, 2 (1960), 329. In 'The Catharsis of *King Lear*', *Shakespeare Survey 13* (1960), p. 1, J. Stampfer noted that Bradley's reading was accepted by Granville-Barker, R. W. Chambers, William Empson, and Kenneth Muir. Among many others who agreed in general with Bradley, including most of those who emphasized the possibilities of Christian allegory, one might note L. C. Knights (*Some Shakespearean Themes*, London, 1959, p. 118) and Harold S. Wilson (*On the Design of Shakespearean Tragedy*, Toronto, 1957, p. 204). For accounts of the varying interpretations of Lear's final lines I am indebted to manuscript essays by R. A. Foakes and David Samuelson.

[3] 'The Figure in Professor Knights's Carpet', *Critical Quarterly*, 2 (1960), 175.

[4] 'Lear's Last Speech', *Shakespeare Survey 13*, p. 17.

[5] ' "Speak What We Feel": The End of *Lear*, ' *English Language Notes*, 5 (1968), 166.

look there!' means primarily 'look upon death', while Thomas Van Laan judges that in the final speeches, 'Lear has completely lost contact with external reality . . . the speeches themselves seem no more than noises forced from him, no more than additional "howls".'[6]

Another group has agreed that Lear's last words may indicate some sort of joy, but hardly a redemptive one. Also in 1960, J. Stampfer remarked, 'The tension here . . . lies between an absolute knowledge that Cordelia is dead, and an absolute inability to accept it. . . . Thus he struggles simultaneously for sanity and for the belief that Cordelia lives. Under the strain of these two irreconcilable psychic needs, his mind simply slips and relaxes into temporary madness.' In contrast to Gloucester, Lear dies 'between extremes of illusion and truth, ecstasy and the blackest despair, at the knowledge that his daughter was needlessly butchered'.[7] Nicholas Brooke thought Cordelia's 'death kills all life'. The end of the play, with Lear's 'final retreat to madness', 'makes it impossible to retain *any* concept of an ordered universe'.[8] John D. Rosenburg saw 'Lear's dying in the deluded hope that Cordelia lives' as 'the last and cruelest of the play's mockeries'.[9] Most of this group, like most of those who reject any notion that the dying Lear feels momentary joy, censured the failings of their predecessors. 'The record', Nicholas Brooke remarked, apparently of nearly all

[6] *Some Facets of 'King Lear': Essays in Prismatic Criticism*, ed. Rosalie L. Colie and F. T. Flahiff (Toronto, 1974), pp. 115, 73-4. Other recent readers have left the question of Lear's final emotion uncertain: Rosalie Colie asked, in the volume cited (p. 192), 'Does Lear die thinking Cordelia dead or alive—can we tell, or should we try to tell?'; Helen Gardner remarked, 'if Bradley is right in thinking that Lear dies in excess of joy because he thinks that breath has stirred on Cordelia's lips, he dies, as he has lived, refusing to accept what all the bystanders know: that Cordelia is dead, and "all's cheerless, dark, and deadly"' (*King Lear*, London, 1967, p. 22); and Northrop Frye, 'Perhaps he thinks that she is coming back to life again, and dies of an unbearable joy. But we do not see this: all we see is an old man dying of an unbearable pain' (*Fools of Time: Studies in Shakespearean Tragedy*, Toronto, 1967, p. 115). Maynard Mack cautiously remarked, 'these lines . . . probably mean that Lear dies in the joy of believing that Cordelia lives' (*'King Lear' in Our Time*, Berkeley', 1965, p. 114).

[7] *Shakespeare Survey 13*, pp. 2-3. 'Relaxes' seems an odd word in relation to Lear's final exclamations, and one wonders whether a human being could be 'needfully butchered'. In *'King Lear' and the Gods* (San Marino, 1966), p. 277, William R. Elton echoed Stampfer's judgement and language.

[8] 'The Ending of *King Lear*', *Shakespeare: 1564-1964*, ed. Edward A. Bloom (Providence, 1964), pp. 84-5.

[9] 'King Lear and His Comforters', *Essays in Criticism*, 16 (1966), 144.

the readings of the play since Dr Johnson's, 'is of a long series of strenuous efforts to circumvent the pain' (p. 77). Rosenburg thought most post-Bradleyan commentary an attempt to 'escape', to 'convert horror into purgation . . . mutilation and murder into salvation' (p. 135). The tone was almost evangelical as the young condemned the old for their failure of nerve, their inability to face reality—the meaningless desolation and despair that are truly 'there'. These critics did not usually consider whether the reality they saw so clearly in the final lines of the play might be conditioned by their own presuppositions and beliefs—although *King Lear* may go farther than any of Shakespeare's plays except *The Tempest* to suggest that ordinarily we see only the reality that we make and share.

I am reluctant, however, to accept the notion that the final lines of *Lear* provide only a mirror for our preconceptions, and I resist the assumption that one reading of *Lear* is as good as another. Some accounts include more of the possibilities of any play than do others; when they do so without obvious distortions or eccentricities, they are usually better than the others. The suggestion that there is nothing in the text which allows us to know what Lear 'sees' limits for the worse the very notion of the 'text'. It may well be that we can determine, in a manner so as to command universal agreement, little or nothing of particular interest concerning either a play of Shakespeare's or a human life; but at least we can make some shrewd guesses concerning probabilities on the basis of the evidence. A text does not imply simply words arranged according to syntactical patterns of sounds and rhythms. In a dramatic text these and other patterns are related to the emotions and actions of individual speakers: they characterize 'persons' and their changing or repetitious responses to experiences, and they suggest relationships between those persons. To read the text is, of course, what we all try to do. The difficulties in reading Shakespeare's texts often derive from the fact that they provide so many and such various possibilities.[10]

[10] Like Bradley's and those of most other readers of the play since the early eighteenth century, my reading of *Lear* was originally based on modern, editorially conflated texts. Recently a number of scholars have argued impressively that both the Quarto and the Folio preserve authoritative dramatic texts, each markedly superior to the usual modern editorial conflation of the two. (See Michael J. Warren, 'Quarto and Folio *King Lear* and the Interpretation of Albany and Edgar', *Shakespeare: Pattern of*

To return to Bradley: if we wish to consider his interpretation of the final lines of Lear, we must go back to what he wrote rather than to unsympathetic summaries:

If to the reader, as to the bystander, that scene brings one unbroken pain, it is not so with Lear himself. His shattered mind passes from the first transports of hope and despair, as he bends over Cordelia's body and holds the feather to her lips, into an absolute forgetfulness of the causes of these transports. This continues so long as he can converse with Kent; becomes an almost complete vacancy; and is disturbed only to yield, as his eyes suddenly fall again on his child's corpse, to agony which at once breaks his heart. And, finally, though he is killed by an agony of pain, the agony in which he actually dies is one not of pain but of ecstasy. Suddenly, with a cry represented in the oldest text by a four-time repeated 'O', he exclaims:

> Do you see this? Look on her, look, her lips,
> Look there, look there!

These are the last words of Lear. He is sure, at last, that she *lives*: and what had he said when he was still in doubt?

> She lives! if it be so,
> It is a chance which does redeem all sorrows
> That ever I have felt!

To us, perhaps, the knowledge that he is deceived may bring a culmination of pain: but, if it brings *only* that, I believe we are false to Shakespeare, and it seems almost beyond question that any actor is false to the text who does not attempt to express, in Lear's last accents and gestures and look, an unbearable *joy*.   (p. 291)

Bradley was reading carefully and imagining a possible performance. He did not, moreover, leave his observation of 'unbearable *joy*' simply as a wayward impression, but supported it with a brief note on the patterning of the last speeches:

This idea may be condemned as fantastic, but the text, it appears to

Excelling Nature, ed. David Bevington and Jay L. Halio, Newark and London, 1978, pp. 95-107; Gary Taylor, 'The War in "King Lear"', *Shakespeare Survey 33* (1980), pp. 27-34; Steven Urkowitz, *Shakespeare's Revision of King Lear*, Princeton, 1980; and Peter W. M. Blayney's *The Texts of 'King Lear' and their Origin*, Vol. i, Cambridge, 1983; Vol. ii forthcoming.) Although I continue to refer throughout to Kenneth Muir's New Arden text (1952; corrected 1955, 1957, 1963), I have attempted to base my central arguments on the Folio, as representing the later as well as better version of the play. Lear's final lines that conclude, 'Look there, look there!' do not appear in the Quarto.

me, will bear no other interpretation. This is the whole speech (in the Globe text):

> And my poor fool is hang'd! No, no, no life!
> Why should a dog, a horse, a rat, have life,
> And thou no breath at all? Thou'lt come no more,
> Never, never, never, never, never!
> Pray you, undo this button: thank you sir.
> Do you see this? Look on her, look, her lips,
> Look there, look there!

The transition at 'Do you see this?' from despair to something more than hope is exactly the same as in the preceding passage at the word 'Ha!':

> A plague upon you, murderers, traitors all!
> I might have saved her; now she's gone for ever!
> Cordelia, Cordelia, stay a little.
> Ha!
> What is't thou say'st? Her voice was ever soft,
> Gentle, and low, an excellent thing in woman.
>
> (pp. 291-2)

In the spacious days of 1904, when he could quote the Globe edition without either line numbers or apology and when he was not particularly concerned with the scholarship or commentary of others, Bradley assumed that the note provided sufficient support or 'proof' of his major point for an intelligent reader. In his perception of the pattern of reversal in Lear's last speeches, he touched on one important kind of evidence which any reader must take into account in trying to determine the meaning or meanings of Shakespeare's texts. He could have cited, had he thought it important or necessary, a number of other passages in support of his interpretation.

The sequence of despairing 'knowledge' of Cordelia's death followed by joyful 'knowledge' of her life actually occurs three times in these final lines.[11] When Lear enters with Cordelia in his arms, he has no doubt of her death and its horror:

> She's gone for ever.
> I know when one is dead, and when one lives;
> She's dead as earth.   (V. iii. 259-61)

---

[11] Carol Marks exactly reverses the sequence: 'three times Lear tests his illusory hope that she lives, and three times hope dies' (*English Language Notes*, 5 (1968), 166).

But his lamentation is interrupted by the possibility of life and breath:

> Lend me a looking-glass;
> If that her breath will mist or stain the stone,
> Why, then she lives.   (261-3)

The scene which seems to Kent and Edgar and Albany the end of the world or an image of its horror is transformed for Lear by a new conviction: 'This feather stirs; she lives!'

The second sequence begins when Lear violently dismisses Kent and Edgar as if their attempts to get his attention had, by interrupting his efforts to revive her, caused Cordelia's death; then immediately changes the tense of completed action for the present as he addresses Cordelia directly: 'Cordelia, Cordelia! stay a little' and 'Ha! / What is't thou say'st?' as he thinks she speaks to him. It seems inconceivable that Shakespeare would have used the pattern twice within sixteen lines had he not intended his audience to understand that in his final lines Lear has again, after full recognition of her death and his own desolation, come to certainty that he sees life in Cordelia's face: 'Do you see this? Look on her, look, her lips, / Look there, look there!'

Bradley's observation that the word 'Ha' marks the transition 'from despair to something more than hope' might also be supported by noting that on the six previous occasions Lear has used that exclamation, 'Ha!' seems always to indicate his astonished recognition of an unexpected or unconfirmed truth.[12] Even when he is maddest, 'Ha' indicates, in addition to pain or surprise or questioning, a degree of satisfaction in what he believes that he has learned.

If Lear sees Cordelia as alive in the final lines, what does it mean? What is the effect—or the possible effects—when Lear's 'sight' is communicated to an audience in the theatre? L. C. Knights spoke for some of the most sensitive commentators when he remarked, 'The scene of Lear's final anguish is so painful that criticism hesitates to fumble with it.'[13] It is easy to go wrong—to push for a kind of clarity and finality that

---

[12] See I. iv. 66, 237, 314; II. iv. 5-6; III. iv. 108-11; IV. vi. 97. The pattern is evident in the Folio; a number of the 'Ha's' do not appear in the Quarto.

[13] *Some Shakespearean Themes*, p. 117.

Shakespeare could have provided but surely did not; and the results of such interpretations can be fairly disastrous in attempts to produce the play on the stage or screen: final concentration on the group of survivors watching the soul of Lear ascend to heaven may be even more distracting than a final lingering on a landscape full of corpses and burning desolation —the world as hell. Clearly, some critics would prefer to the figure in the final lines what they think of as a more heroic Lear: one who died utterly lucid, recognizing all the quotidian reality that the spectators do, and perhaps even cursing the heavens and the gods for the meaningless and cruel universe over which they preside—or fail to preside. Whatever our desires, if we wish to understand Shakespeare's play, we must consider the final lines in relation both to the character of Lear as it has been developed from the beginning and to the play as a whole.

From the opening scene, when his intended bestowal of the 'third more opulent than your sisters' (I. i. 86) upon Cordelia is suddenly transformed by Cordelia's repeated 'Nothing' into his awful disowning of her, Lear's most terrible and poignant moments are marked by sudden reversals of beliefs and emotions and determinations. In the opening scene Lear assumes knowledge. When his assumptions, beliefs, 'certainties' are suddenly opposed or shattered, he responds first with incredulity and then with rage and a pronouncement of banishment or a curse. That pattern, continually repeated, becomes more and more painful as it is crossed by other patterns of emotional response in which Lear attempts to conquer sorrow and tears by 'manliness' and noble anger by patience, only to have all dissolve in rage, the desire to kill and destroy, and, finally, madness. One of the things that make these changes so painful is that Lear's responses are open, exclamatory, and repetitious, and that he early comes to recognize his own guilt and folly:

> O Lear, Lear, Lear!
> Beat at this gate, that let thy folly in,
> [*Striking his head*
> And thy dear judgment out!
> (I. iv. 279-81)

His pleas for patience and attempts at control are not mere

efforts to retain dignity or propriety or even clarity of judgement, but desperate attempts to forestall the madness that he
feels approach in the waves of his overwhelming emotions:

> O! let me not be mad, not mad, sweet heaven . . .   (I. v. 47)

These conflicting patterns become particularly oppressive in
Act II, scene iv, from the moment when Lear insists that the
reasons Kent gives for being in the stocks could not be true:

> *Lear.* What's he that hath so much thy place mistook
>   To set thee here?
> *Kent.*   It is both he and she,
>   Your son and daughter.
> *Lear.* No.
> *Kent.* Yes.
> *Lear.* No, I say.
> *Kent.* I say, yea.
> *Lear.* No, no; they would not.
> *Kent.* Yes, they have.
> *Lear.* By Jupiter, I swear, no.
> *Kent.* By Juno, I swear, ay.
> *Lear.*   They durst not do't,
>   They could not, would not do't; tis worse than murther,
>   To do upon respect such violent outrage.   (12-24)

After hearing Kent's account, Lear has a moment when,
almost overcome by his emotion, he attempts to control it just
before he exits:

> O! how this mother swells up toward my heart;
> *Hysterica passio!* down, thou climbing sorrow!
> Thy element's below. Where is this daughter?
>   (56-8)

On his return, Lear is incensed by Gloucester's remark about
the 'fiery quality' of Cornwall: in his repeated exclamations
rage begins to predominate over incredulity:

> *Lear.* Vengeance! plague! death! confusion!
>   Fiery! what quality? Why Gloucester, Gloucester,
>   I'd speak with the Duke of Cornwall and his wife.
> *Gloucester.* Well, my good Lord, I have inform'd them so.
> *Lear.* Inform'd them! Dost thou understand me, man?
> *Gloucester.* Ay, my good Lord.   (95-100)

In the next speech, Lear, beginning with outrage, makes an enormous effort at control, imaginative sympathy with Regan and Cornwall, and even critical judgement on himself; but it is all swept away by the renewed sight of Kent, his messenger, still sitting in the stocks. It is after Goneril and Regan's public competition to show least love ('What need one?') that the struggles between contradictory emotions become literally unbearable, and Lear comes to the certainty that madness lies ahead.

In the storm the Gentleman tells Kent that Lear is 'Contending with the fretful elements':

> Bids the wind blow the earth into the sea,
> Or swell the curled waters 'bove the main,
> That things might change or cease . . .
> (III. i. 5-7)

When we see Lear, however, his commands and invocations entertain more limited alternatives: he bids things to cease, to be made manifest, and to be judged; and in the first storm scene Lear uses none of those doubled words and phrases which have characterized his excited speech of discovery until then. It is in III. iv, with 'Poor Tom's' 'Fathom and half, fathom and half!' (III. iv. 37) that the emotional repetitions are introduced again as Edgar, the Fool, and Lear exchange the language and cries of madness:

Fool. Help me! help me!   (40)

Fool. A spirit, a spirit.   (42)

Edgar. O! do de, do de, do de.   (58-9)

Edgar. There could I have him now, and there, and there again, and there.   (61-2)

Edgar. Alow, alow, loo, loo!   (77)

Edgar. Dolphin my boy, boy . . .   (101-2)

Lear. Off, off, you lendings!   (111)

Edgar. And aroint thee, witch, aroint thee!   (127)

Edgar. Peace, Smulkin! peace, thou fiend!   (144-5)

In III. vi, the repetitions resume with Lear's answer to the Fool's riddle about whether a madman is a gentleman or a yeoman:

Lear. A King, a King!   (11)

Lear. Arms, arms, sword, fire!   (55)

Edgar. Do de, de, de.   (74)

Lear. so, so.   (86)

Edgar. Lurk, lurk.   (118)

Lear's maddened, repeated cries reach a climax in Act IV, scene vi, the scene where he meets the blinded Gloucester:

O! well flown bird; i' th' clout, i' th' clout: hewgh!   (92-3)

fie, fie, fie! pah, pah!   (131)

None does offend, none, I say, none; I'll able 'em:
Take that of me, my friend, who have the power
To seal th' accuser's lips. Get thee glass eyes,
And, like a scurvy politician, seem
To see the things thou dost not. Now, now, now, now;
Pull off my boots; harder, harder; so.   (170-5)

After 'preaching' to Gloucester of the necessity for patience (here, seemingly, merely endurance), Lear's effort to give a despairing universal pardon to all offenders dissolves into the desire to kill:

It were a delicate stratagem to shoe
A troop of horse with felt; I'll put 't in proof,
And when I have stol'n upon these son-in-laws,
Then kill, kill, kill, kill, kill, kill!   (186-9)

Anne Barton has remarked, 'Not, I think, by accident, are repeated words so characteristic of this tragedy. The last two acts are filled with frenzied repetitions, some of them hammered upon as many as six times in the course of a single line: "Kill," "Now," "Howl," "Never," the monosyllabic "No." One comes to feel that these words are being broken on the anvil in an effort to determine whether or not there is anything inside.' Barton relates these repetitions to the broken syntax and the general inadequacy of language: 'There is no vocabulary for what [Lear] feels.' 'Words define the gap between individuals; they do not bridge it.'[14] Although her formulations

---

[14] 'Shakespeare and the Limits of Language', *Shakespeare Survey 24* (1971), pp. 19-27. The repetitions are more striking in the Folio than in the Quarto. Winifred M. T. Nowottny had earlier made a similar point: 'Shakespeare concentrates upon Lear the

are attractive and moving, I think they are also overstated and partial. Not unless we limit language to the clearly denotative or to rational or conceptual propositions or to standard and conventional speech patterns can we maintain that the language of *King Lear* is in any sense inadequate. Those impassioned repetitions are related to Shakespeare's 'unprecedented insistence' in *Lear* 'that the audience actively participate in the emotional experience of his characters'.[15] If at times we feel the enormous gaps between individuals, at other times the language creates, as it explores the limits of human experience, remarkable 'bridges', both between the characters on the stage and between them and the members of the audience.

We can understand and respond to Lear's incredulous, exclamatory, and mad repetitions partly because the speeches of the other characters create a fabric of analogous and contrasting meanings, a 'language' we learn within the course of the play. Beginning with 'Let's see, let's see' as he starts to peruse Edmund's forged letter (I. ii. 44), Gloucester's early repeated exclamations—simple-minded, a bit self-important, turning to the histrionic in sentimental self-pity—are pale foreshadowings of Lear's later anguish:

O villain, villain! His very opinion in the letter! Abhorred villain! Unnatural, detested, brutish villain! worse than brutish! Go, sirrah, seek him; I'll apprehend him. Abominable villain!   (I. ii. 75-9)

> O! Madam, my old heart is crack'd, it's crack'd.   (II. i. 90)
>
> O! Lady, Lady, shame would have it hid.   (II. i. 93)
>
> I know not, Madam; 'tis too bad, too bad.   (II. i. 96)

Edmund parodies his father's melodramatic urgency when he stage-manages his pretended struggle with Edgar: 'Torches! torches! . . . Father! father! / Stop, stop! No help?' (II. i. 33-7). But we have heard Edmund's more natural mode of

style that gives a felt experience of the incommensurateness of human nature to what it must endure. . . . The play is deeply concerned with the inadequacy of language to do justice to feeling or to afford any handhold against abysses of iniquity and suffering. . . . [Lear] must use language not as the adequate register of experience, but as evidence that his experience is beyond language's scope' ('Some Aspects of the Style of *King Lear*', *Shakespeare Survey 13* (1960), pp. 51-3).

15 Nancy R. Lindheim, '*King Lear* as Pastoral Tragedy', *Some Facets of 'King Lear'*, p. 174.

thought and speech in his first soliloquy in which, with cool and playful malevolence, he contemplated the doubleness of language and value. It is Edmund who tests, to see 'whether or not there is anything inside', the words which ordinarily indicate familial relationships, legal judgements, and moral values:

> Why brand they us
> With base? with baseness? bastardy? base, base?
> Who in the lusty stealth of nature take
> More composition and fierce quality
> Than doth, within a dull, stale, tired bed,
> Go to th' creating a whole tribe of fops,
> Got 'tween asleep and wake? Well then,
> Legitimate Edgar, I must have your land:
> Our father's love is to the bastard Edmund
> As to th' legitimate. Fine word, "legitimate"!
> Well, my legitimate, if this letter speed,
> And my invention thrive, Edmund the base
> Shall top th' legitimate—: I grow, I prosper;
> Now, gods, stand up for bastards!   (I. ii. 9-22)

In Regan's and Cornwall's repetitions, anger and absolute insistence on their own power and purposes leave little room for any other emotion; impulses toward playfulness are lost in the ingenuities of cruelty:

> *Cornwall.*   Fetch forth the stocks!
>   As I have life and honour, there shall he sit till noon.
> *Regan.* Till noon! till night, my Lord; and all night too.
>   (II. ii. 133-5)
> *Cornwall.* Bind him, I say.
> *Regan.* Hard, hard. O filthy traitor!   (III. vii. 32)
> *Cornwall.* Where hast thou sent the King?
> *Gloucester.*   To Dover.
> *Regan.* Wherefore to Dover? Wast thou not charg'd at peril—
> *Cornwall.* Wherefore to Dover? Let him answer that.
> *Gloucester.* I am tied to th' stake, and I must stand the course.
> *Regan.* Wherefore to Dover?   (III. vii. 50-4)

To these and the following horrible repetitions of 'see', Edgar's cry, 'World, world, O world!' (IV. i. 10) may seem the inevitable response of astonishment and defeat.

It is, of course, Cordelia whose language is able to still Lear's anguished repetitions and to end the storm within him.

When we see her again in IV. iv her manner and language are precisely as the Gentleman had described them in the Quarto's IV. iii.[16] Her shock, incredulity, and grief are free from Lear's rage, guilt, and attempts at 'noble anger', as well as his despair, desire to kill, and madness. All of her emotions are compatible with love. She ends scene iv with an apostrophe:

> O dear father!
> It is thy business that I go about;
> Therefore great France
> My mourning and importun'd tears hath pitied.
> No blown ambition doth our arms incite,
> But love, dear love, and our ag'd father's right.
> Soon may I hear and see him!   (IV. iv. 23-9)

The final half-line, coming surprisingly after the conclusive couplet, is very moving.[17]

It is important that we hear Cordelia's cadences when we do, but Lear does not hear the voice that ends his nausea and madness until Act IV, scene vii, when he wakes to a kiss, and discovers his royal robes restored and a daughter who weeps and kneels. He thought he had come to know the truth of life—his life—that it was a hell of torment; Cordelia's face (which he had sworn he would never see again), her kiss, and her words ('How does my royal Lord? How fares your Majesty?') convince him that she cannot be living in his realm. Lear's struggle to discover where he is, whether he is asleep, whether he can trust his senses (his questions concern always not what he can 'believe' but what he can 'know'—the difference is that between speculative commitment in a realm that leaves room for contemplative mental distance and total imaginative certainty within the present moment of a life of suffering),[18] is inter-

---

[16] A production which follows the Folio in omitting Act IV, scene iii, with its unusually rhetorical Gentleman, seriously weakens the role of Cordelia.

[17] Shakespeare may have remembered a similar cadence, coupled with love and the desire to aid and a prayer, at the end of an earlier scene in the Quarto, when the Third Servant moved to comfort the blind Gloucester:

> Go thou; I'll fetch some flax and whites of eggs
> To apply to his bleeding face. Now, heaven help him!
>   (III. vii. 105-6)

[18] William R. Elton, by contrast, thinks that 'King Lear's ultimate question' is 'What can man believe?' (*'King Lear' and the Gods*, p. 62). He reads the play as primarily concerned with questioning religious belief.

rupted when Cordelia kneels to ask his blessing. After his immediate attempt to kneel to her, he confesses his foolishness, age, doubtful sanity, and ignorance, and he ventures the *thought* that 'this lady' is Cordelia. Cordelia's repeated assurance ('And so I am, I am') does not go all the way to convince Lear that his former hard-earned knowledge of the world's reality was incomplete. He had thought that, while daughters might speak the language of love when they had none in their hearts and while one might well be recompensed for the gift of a kingdom with hatred and attempts on one's life, good, at least, must be significantly related to, if not identical with, justice: a recognition of, and either reward or punishment for, remarkable deservings. He assumes that Cordelia's tears are marks of remorse for the 'just' punishment which she must, since she is good, intend to inflict upon him for his wrongs to her:

> Be your tears wet? Yes, faith. I pray, weep not:
> If you have poison for me, I will drink it.
> I know you do not love me; for your sisters
> Have, as I do remember, done me wrong:
> You have some cause, they have not.   (71-5)

From Cordelia's 'No cause, no cause', Lear makes a discovery more astonishing than any of the earlier ones: love is as gratuitous as evil; it has nothing to do with deservings; it is long suffering and kind, returns good for evil, and perceives 'no cause' for hatred or revenge.

When we next see Lear, he has fully understood. He is utterly unconcerned with the military defeat, utterly indifferent to being king. His exclamatory repetitions are now reserved to ward off Cordelia's suggestion that they should see 'these daughters and these sisters': 'No, no, no, no! Come, let's away to prison; / We two alone will sing like birds i' th' cage' (V. iii. 8-9). Lear's joy is absolute. He is so sure that he and Cordelia are above and beyond the times and tides that govern the powers of this world that he can imagine them only as pastimes for their amused conversation and contemplation.

Bradley remarked, 'I might almost say that the "moral" of *King Lear* is presented in the irony of this collocation:

> *Albany.* The gods defend her!
> *Enter Lear with Cordelia dead in his arms.*

The "gods," it seems, do *not* show their approval by "defend-ing" their own from adversity or death, or by giving them power and prosperity.'[19] As excruciating as it is, I think one can imagine more horrible endings than the one Shakespeare gives us—a view of Goneril triumphant, say, perhaps subject-ing Cordelia and Lear to slow torture, looking forward to a long rule with her consort Edmund. It would be even more ter-rible if Cordelia changed and lived to scorn Lear—or even if Lear in his madness thought she did. But such changes would require a change of the principal emphasis of the play from the fate of Lear or inconsistent shifts in the natures of the major characters. One can hardly believe that any of the predators could live long in each other's presence, and what we have heard and seen of Cordelia will not allow us to imagine that her love could change. Granted that the ending must give a sense of completion to the tragedy of *Lear*, Shakespeare's ending seems as painful as one can imagine.

Bradley remarked that, with the ending, 'It is as if Shake-speare said to us: "Did you think weakness and innocence have any chance here? Were you beginning to dream that? I will show you it is not so." '[20] Paul Jorgensen has remarked that Lear's ultimate question 'will no longer be, Who loves me most? but rather, Of what final reassurance is even true love? or, more urgently, What am I if Cordelia is nothing?'[21] and we are drawn into personally anguished involvement with those questions, too. Our attempts to preserve some comfortable dis-tance from the characters, particularly the usual tendency to resist the threats of tragic suffering by clinging to the sense of our spectator's or reader's superior moral perceptions, or

---

[19] *Shakespearean Tragedy*, p. 326. Winifred M. T. Nowottny noted meanings which 'this collocation' suggests beyond Bradley's 'moral': 'Along the receding planes keyed into this tableau we see in an instant of time Lear's sin and its retribution, the wider evil that has struck both, the full fatherhood of Lear bearing his child in his arms whilst at the same time the natural course of life is seen reversed (Lear senile, so lately cared for by Cordelia), the world's destruction of the love and forgiveness that had transcended it—for the reverberation of the reunion is still strong and the language of that scene has opened the way to those suggestions of a saviour's death which now make it inescapable that Cordelia dead in her father's arms and displayed to the world, should strike deeply into responses that lie midway between religion and art' (*Shakespeare Survey 13* (1960), p. 56).

[20] *Shakespearean Tragedy*, p. 271.

[21] *Lear's Self-Discovery* (Berkeley and Los Angeles, 1967), p. 99.

imagination, or knowledge, or at least alertness, have been subtly undermined, I believe, by what has happened to our attention in the long and intricate final scene. We in the audience are immediately concerned with the fates of Cordelia and Lear when the Officer who has agreed to carry out Edmund's orders follows them to prison; but we do not hear the details of the orders, and during the crowded sequence of events which follows (the confrontations between Albany, Edmund, and Regan, the challenge and the herald's trumpet, the appearance of the armed and helmeted Edgar and the duel, the mortal wounding of Edmund, the 'discovery' of Edgar and his narration of the death of Gloucester, the messenger's announcement of the deaths of Goneril and Regan), we are largely concerned with other things. I believe most members of the audience are doubly moved by Albany's conscience-stricken response to Kent's inquiry for Lear, 'Great thing of us forgot!' (236). We too had momentarily forgotten, and we can hardly believe it possible that we should have done so. We have shared to some degree in the awful carelessness or distraction among the well-intentioned which causes or allows or at least ignores disaster, and with weakened defences we share with the other survivors the ultimate question of the play: what if, after wrongs and loss and agony, recognition and the acquisition of knowledge and the discovery of love, one found murdered the one who embodied all that one had come to know and love? Could anything make us feel at such a moment that life was worth living?

If at the end we respond to Lear's death as heroic rather than merely pathetic, it is, I believe, because his final powerful fluctuating responses cast doubt on the 'realities' which we often assume as objective or self-evident—even on the question of what we mean by 'life'. What Lear wills or desires is less important than what he perceives and 'knows'. Those repeated 'howls' at his entrance express his immediate response to his *knowledge* that Cordelia is dead:

> Howl, howl, howl! O! you are men of stones:
> Had I your tongue and eyes, I'd use them so
> That heaven's vault should crack. She's gone for ever.
> I know when one is dead, and when one lives;
> She's dead as earth.   (257-61)

His request for the looking-glass, which directly follows, indicates his inability to believe that the face on which he gazes is
without life. It is neither weak nor mad, but a fairly common
experience in the first moments or hours after death—particularly when there are neither physicians nor machines to
give assurance of what the eyes alone cannot determine—for
the survivors who gaze on the faces of those they have loved to
believe that they can see signs of life within them. 'This feather
stirs' almost certainly reports what the feather does do when it
is held tightly in a trembling hand and observed closely. Lear
takes the 'stirring' as evidence of a redeeming possibility.

> This feather stirs; she lives! if it be so,
> It is a chance which does redeem all sorrows
> That ever I have felt.   (265-7)

Lear brushes Kent and the others roughly aside when Kent
kneels and seeks for recognition, acknowledgement, and a farewell:

> A plague upon you, murderers, traitors all!
> I might have sav'd her; now she's gone for ever!
> Cordelia, Cordelia! stay a little. Ha!
> What is't thou say'st? Her voice was ever soft,
> Gentle and low, an excellent thing in woman.
> I kill'd the slave that was a-hanging thee.
>   (269-74)

The shifts of tense and address are both astonishing and moving. After line 270, with its assumption that Cordelia is already
dead ('she's gone for ever'), Lear addresses Cordelia with the
plea, 'stay a little', as if only a slight delay in her departure
would be enough, anticipating Kent's later assuredness in 'I
have a journey, sir, shortly to go': for these two, as for Hamlet
after his return from the voyage for England, the knowledge
that the interval will be brief makes the precise time of death
relatively unimportant. Lear's 'Ha!' marks the moment of a
new 'discovery', when he thinks that Cordelia is speaking to
him. He has learned that he can no longer trust his senses for a
full or accurate account of external reality. At the beginning of
the play he had heard and believed the words of Goneril and
Regan and he had heard and failed to understand those of

Cordelia. These and later 'crosses' have provided Lear with an experiential basis for profound scepticism concerning his perceptions. So now he believes that she *is* speaking to him and that it is only her 'soft, / Gentle and low' voice that prevents him from hearing precisely words, the emotional import of which he is sure—since they come from Cordelia. The question, 'What is't thou say'st?' is addressed directly to Cordelia; the description of her voice, to those surrounding figures who were just before dismissed (with all the world) as murderers and traitors. With the last sentence, 'I kill'd the slave that was a-hanging thee', he addresses Cordelia once again, telling her of the one recent event she may not have known.[22]

When the Officer confirms his statement, Lear for the first time truly notices those around him. He hesitantly recognizes Kent, but he cannot follow the news that Kent and his 'servant Caius' were the same man, and he agrees without interest or knowledge that his eldest daughters 'have fordone themselves, / And desperately are dead' (291-2). From line 274, he seems distracted from the reality of Cordelia's body, but he cannot be much interested in those other persons and events. It is during Albany's speech (295-304) that Lear must again become conscious of the dead Cordelia, and with some sort of paroxysm that elicits Albany's 'O! see, see!' Lear is once again sure of her death:

> And my poor fool is hang'd! No, no, no life!
> Why should a dog, a horse, a rat, have life,
> And thou no breath at all? Thou'lt come no more,
> Never, never, never, never, never!   (305-8)

Lear's former convictions that 'she lives' and that she spoke to him, are rejected either as illusions or as possibilities now past. With that conviction, 'Pray you, undo this button' seems to indicate that, once again, 'this mother' swells up toward his

---

[22] In his effort to demonstrate that Lear has learned nothing and that there is no consolation of any kind at the end of the play, W. R. Elton argues that Lear not only fails in the *ars moriendi* but also ends with 'defiance of the heavens, commission of a confirmed murder . . . and a final heroic vaunt' (*'King Lear' and the Gods*, p. 259). I know of no generally accepted usage of the word 'murder', legal or moral, past or present, that would justify its application to Lear's killing of the 'slave that was a-hanging' Cordelia. It is difficult to imagine an ethical standard (except a totally pacifist one hardly envisaged in the play) by which the action could be censured.

heart and that he is almost suffocated by his emotion and the attendant rush of blood.

But after the touchingly ceremonial 'thank you, Sir' to the character who has helped him undo the button, Lear turns back to Cordelia with, once again, a new and opposite conviction, this time an overwhelming and final one:

> Do you see this? Look on her, look, her lips,
> Look there, look there! (310-11)

If one insists, hard-headedly, that it is sheer delusion, one may still consider it a consummation devoutly to be wished: to die in the conviction that one's dearest loved one is not, as one had thought, dead, but alive. But beyond this, Lear's final convictions that Cordelia is alive and that her lips move are overwhelming recognition of the reality that he has come to know: that the things he has learned from Cordelia about the nature of love (what he has come to perceive as Cordelia's astonishing essence) are more truly alive than anything else in his world. Cordelia's lips speak at this moment more than any other human lips he could ever imagine.[23] Lear had earlier asked Cordelia, 'Have I caught thee?' His last lines indicate that he has indeed, in a sense he had hardly anticipated, by the depth of his unbearably joyful knowledge of a reality and truth that triumph over death and fate and time.

That, I think, is what Lear 'sees', but not what we non-heroic survivors see—except in glimpses of his vision. The monsters may be dead and Lear's sufferings ended, but we may almost envy Lear his passionate certainty. We are left, as often in tragedy, with our eyes directed towards the mortal remains of a figure or figures whose heroic stature is beyond us. We are, moreover, denied even the relative consolation of the usual gestures towards the re-establishment of order. No more than Albany or Kent or Edgar can we care much about promises of continuity and renewal of the state or social fabric. Albany, not wishing to rule, attempts to give the kingdom to Kent and Edgar. When Kent refuses, with the simple reminder that he must shortly follow his master on his last journey, Edgar (if we

---

[23] Sigurd Burckhardt wrote, 'He ends, it might seem, where Gloster, with his "Let's see," began. But he dies believing that he has seen living breath, not letters—words, not signs' (*Shakespearean Meanings*, Princeton, 1968, p. 258).

accept the Folio reading) concludes the play. We may, if we wish, assume that he will accede to Albany's request—that he is the new king, but he does not clearly state this decision. He only remarks that at this moment noble characters no longer speak according to their social and political, or even moral responsibilities, and he acknowledges that 'we that are young' will not (by implication *could* not) survive such suffering—or such joys—as those we have witnessed.

VI

A Definition of Love:
Antony and Cleopatra

There is little general agreement about the nature and success of *Antony and Cleopatra*.[1] Although Coleridge called it 'of all perhaps of Shakespeare's plays the most wonderful',[2] a number of readers have had grave reservations, and nearly all have recognized certain problems, the chief of which concerns the unity of the drama: how can we respond to the action as a whole? Those who dislike the play tend to emphasize the initial degradation of the lovers and to find the nobility of the last scenes unconvincing. Many admirers reverse the process, and are so moved by the final scenes that they attempt to find nobility and transcendence in the earlier scenes as well. Others attempt to bridge the disparities by reading almost everything in the play in an ironic light. S. L. Bethell remarked, 'It remains true that regarding the play psychologically, one cannot reconcile the vicious, the vulgar, and the commonplace in Antony and Cleopatra with the sublimity with which they are invested, especially as they face defeat and death', and his solution was somehow to 'begin—and end—with the poetry itself'.[3] But I think it unsatisfactory to assume an absolute separation of the 'poetry' and the characterization and plot in Shakespeare's poetic dramas, and I also do not believe that the recognition of irony is the major response demanded of his tragedies. Good readers have often compounded the difficulties of this play, as

[1] Janet Adelman's *The Common Liar: An Essay on 'Antony and Cleopatra'* (New Haven and London, 1973) provided a generally comprehensive account of critical responses to the play. (My essay was conceived and substantially written before I read Adelman's stimulating study.) L. T. Fitz's 'Egyptian Queens and Male Reviewers: Sexist Attitudes in *Antony and Cleopatra* Criticism', *Shakespeare Quarterly*, 28 (1977), 297-316, gives a devastating account of masculine treatments of Cleopatra and the play.
[2] *Coleridge's Shakespeare Criticism*, ed. Thomas Middleton Raysor (London, 1930), i. 86.
[3] *Shakespeare and the Popular Dramatic Tradition* (London, 1944), p. 117.

of *Julius Caesar*, in attempts to achieve a consistent (even if 'bal-
anced' or ironic) view of the protagonists, as if they were essentially the same throughout, while in fact the major characters
undergo profound changes within the course of the play, and
the audience is invited (almost compelled) to remarkable
changes in sympathies and judgements as the action unfolds.
Of course there are continuities, and complex judgements are
continually evoked. But to attempt at every moment in the play
to be conscious of all the other or final judgements which we
remember or anticipate from previous readings is to refuse to
submit ourselves to its primary experience: the sequence of
visions and revisions, events and judgements, as they unfold in
a theatrical performance within time.

The play concerns most of Shakespeare's usual themes and
some peculiar ones: man and woman, love and honour (both
public and private), youth and age (and dotage), lust and politics, sensual sloth and heroic action, discipline and licence,
reason and passion. These elements do not exist alone or as
mere polarities, but are played out against other, more particular images of the world: Rome and Egypt (historical empires
and civilizations implying rival ways of life, alive in the play
both as ideals and as degenerate realities), and a range of
mythological presences—Mars and Venus, who regain their
dignity as immortal gods of war and love despite their exposure
to ridicule and shame in the net of Vulcan; Hercules, in strength
a demigod, found effeminately 'among the women' with Om-
phale, and the recipient of the 'intolerable shirt of flame' from
Deianeira; the Dido and Aeneas who Antony imagines will lose
their troop of admirers in the underworld to the new lovers;
and, of course, Circe. And, except for Circe, each of those
figures seems less important as an embodiment of abstract
emotion or action or strength than as an 'unfortunate lover'
who, after incidents or a life involving shame or suffering or
loss, somehow 'climbs' 'To make impression upon time'.[4] The
stage of the play is the world—in no other play of Shakespeare's
does that metaphor become so literally alive. And while the
play recounts actual events from historical time, weeks or

---

[4] Andrew Marvell, 'The Unfortunate Lover'. *Poems and Letters*, ed. H. M.
Margoliouth, 3rd edn. (Oxford, 1971), i. 29.

months or even years of Roman action may pass while only moments occur in Egypt, and the final action moves towards a timeless realm without movement.

At the beginning of the play Philo and Demetrius, two of Antony's relatively anonymous (and therefore, in Shakespearian drama, relatively trustworthy) soldiers, direct our attention, like the figures in the foreground of a large Renaissance painting, to the dotage of a general, a Mars who has abandoned all 'wars without doors', a decayed sensualist who has met his match in Cleopatra. Philo describes to Demetrius the reduction of Antony's 'captain's heart' to the present 'bellows and the fan / To cool a gipsy's lust', and offers the entrance of the lovers as evidence:

> Look, where they come:
> Take but good note, and you shall see in him
> The triple pillar of the world transform'd
> Into a strumpet's fool: behold and see.
> (I. i. 10-15)[5]

At the end of the scene, Demetrius accepts what he has seen and heard as proof of what he did not wish to believe:

> I am full sorry
> That he approves the common liar, who
> Thus speaks of him at Rome; but I will hope
> Of better deeds to-morrow.   (59-62)

By the time of his death Antony has recovered his lost heroism, become a superior Hercules who, despite sufferings, has triumphed in love. In the last Act, within the language of Cleopatra, Antony achieves full apotheosis; and Cleopatra, without ever denying herself or Egypt, both claims and acts upon Roman virtues: she unites the emotions of a milkmaid with the most royal temperament, marble constancy with fire and air; and she becomes the image (both visual and metaphorical) of a transcendent Venus who has triumphed over suffering and time. Of all the plays in which Shakespeare presented dramatic changes in central characters and worked for remarkable shifts in the sympathies of his audience, surely the changes (and the

---

[5] All of my quotations from the play are from the Arden text edited by M. R. Ridley (London, 1954).

chances) are greatest here—and in some respects, so are the rewards.

How is it managed? If the play does not fall apart, how is it kept together? Is it only a matter of metaphor and language, or of a single stage and the same actors? I have already suggested a number of the thematic, mythical, symbolic, and metaphoric elements that I think important: to try fully to demonstrate how they contribute to a triumph of poetic drama would require at least a volume. I wish here to emphasize only one element of the complex structure, less exotic than the experiences of Roman heroes, Egyptian queens, and mythological figures (although closely related to them) and often overlooked: the tradition and the realities of the heterosexual wars. Modern readers may need to be reminded of the common Renaissance notion that lust results in sensual sloth while love leads towards heroic action;[6] but we are all surely familiar with the problematic distinctions between masculine and feminine roles, and probably most of us would agree that lust seeks only to possess and to be possessed, while love implies also a care for another's life and welfare—even beyond one's own life. In the sexual battles and the transformation of lust into heroic love which make up, I believe, the primary action of the play, the lovers achieve their miracle not at all by abandoning sexuality but by committing themselves to their loves, ultimately uniting Roman and Egyptian values in their pristine brightness. Bradley thought we are saddened 'by the very fact that the catastrophe saddens us so little'.[7] He was correct, I believe, in his observation that sadness is not the primary response to the final scenes, but wrong to be disturbed by it, for we can hardly be distressed by the restoration before our eyes of heroic images long tarnished and formerly known only by descriptions or by laments for their loss. Instead of worrying that the ending of *Antony and Cleopatra* differs so much in tone from the endings of *Romeo and Juliet* and *Othello* and *Macbeth*, we might more profit-

---

[6] This commonplace of Ariosto, Tasso, and Spenser underlies Milton's use of the Circe myth from 'Lycidas' to *Samson Agonistes*.

[7] 'Shakespeare's *Antony and Cleopatra*', *Oxford Lectures on Poetry* (London, 1909), p. 304.

ably notice some of the ways in which it anticipates the ending of *The Winter's Tale*.[8]

To return to the opening scene: Philo and Demetrius do not merely see Antony as a hero who has abandoned military action and the greater world of Rome for Egypt and love; they see him as both fool and slave of passion, a parody of the dominated male. Just after Philo has described Antony's 'great captain's heart' reduced to 'the bellows and the fan / To cool a gipsy's lust', we see in the ceremonial procession of the lovers and their attendants that it is Cleopatra's eunuchs who literally fan her, while Antony shows his subservience in other gestures and speech. That shocking suggestion of a true relation between the boasted sexual powers of the enthralled lover and impotence is further developed in the play. It reflects the paradoxical insight of the Circe myth: those enchanted by Circe are reduced to less than men, beasts totally within the power of another; however they may rejoice in their state, they have lost their freedom and individuality; and however much Circe asserts her power over them, there is little question of her 'loving' them—or even being satisfied by them for long.

Although by the end of the play we may see new meanings in Antony's boasts of the transcendental power of his love ('then must thou needs find out new heaven, new earth,' he tells Cleopatra, if she is to 'set a bourn how far to be belov'd'—I. i. 16-17), in the opening scene they are evidences of Cleopatra's sovereignty over Antony. She begins with 'If it be love indeed, tell me how much' (14), but she does not for a moment make Lear's mistake of thinking that love can be proven by public words; her question is simply a gambit, part of her amused and comic demonstration of how she can 'play' Antony. A high point of the comedy comes in scene iii, when for almost thirty lines she prevents Antony from completing the sentence which would announce his departure for Rome.

Later, in Antony's absence, Cleopatra tells Mardian she

---

[8] In *Shakespearean Tragedy*, pp. 83-4, Bradley contrasted *Antony and Cleopatra* and *Coriolanus* with his four central tragedies in that they do not 'display . . . extreme forms of evil' and none of their characters 'can be called villainous or horrible'. Both end, moreover, with a sense of 'reconciliation'. Bradley anticipated my suggestion about *Antony and Cleopatra* when he remarked that at the 'close of *Coriolanus* we feel, it seems to me, more as we do at the close of *Cymbeline* than as we do at the close of *Othello*'.

takes 'no pleasure / In aught an eunuch has' (I. v. 9-10), yet
in the early part of the play she often reduces Antony to something like one. In the great gap of time of Antony's absence,
she remarks to Mardian,

> Give me mine angle, we'll to the river there,
> My music playing far off. I will betray
> Tawny-finn'd fishes, my bended hook shall pierce
> Their slimy jaws; and as I draw them up,
> I'll think them every one an Antony,
> And say, 'Ah, ha! y'are caught.'   (II. v. 10-15)

And she remembers past times when

> I laugh'd him out of patience; and that night
> I laugh'd him into patience, and next morn,
> Ere the ninth hour, I drunk him to his bed;
> Then put my tires and mantles on him, whilst
> I wore his sword Philippan.   (19-23)

Her description provides precise and imaginatively convincing
images for Caesar's charge that Antony 'is not more manlike /
Than Cleopatra; nor the queen of Ptolemy / More womanly
than he' (I. iv. 5-7).

Yet Cleopatra's efforts to assert and test her power over
Antony stem at least partly from her uncertainty of his love.
After Antony has at last received the Roman messengers, Cleo-
patra sends Alexas to find him:

> See where he is, who's with him, what he does:
> I did not send you. If you find him sad,
> Say I am dancing; if in mirth, report
> That I am sudden sick. Quick, and return.
>   (I. iii. 2-5)

Charmian protests that if Cleopatra 'did love him dearly, / You
do not hold the method, to enforce / The like from him' (6-8),
and advises that she should 'In each thing give him way, cross
him in nothing'. Cleopatra replies scornfully, 'Thou teachest
like a fool: the way to lose him', and she speaks from long
experience of successfully controlled masculine infatuations.
But Charmian's warning is significant:

> Tempt him not so too far. I wish, forbear;
> In time we hate that which we often fear.
>   (11-12)

For Antony does fear her, and at this point the enchantment seems to work only when he is in her presence. Alone or with other Romans he feels his nature as man, warrior, and ruler threatened by her, and he early resolves, 'These strong Egyptian fetters I must break, / Or lose myself in dotage' (I. ii. 113-14). In her absence he can even say, 'Would I had never seen her' (I. ii. 150); but when he is with her he insists that he goes from her 'Thy soldier, servant, making peace or war, / As thou affects' (I. iii. 69-71), and that his love 'stands / An honourable trial' (74-5). At the moment he makes that speech, I do not believe either Antony or we can tell whether he is lying. Cleopatra assumes he is and encourages his performance with 'Good now, play one scene / Of excellent dissembling, and let it look / Like perfect honour' (78-80); when he remains determined to return to Rome, there is one moment when she passionately confesses her fear that in the decision he has already abandoned her ('O, my oblivion is a very Antony, / And I am all forgotten'—90-1), before she recovers and achieves a fully Roman farewell.

When alone, Antony imagines his return to Rome precisely as a recovery of the 'self', an affirmation of responsible action against enslaved self-indulgence. But when we see him in Rome, fencing politically with Caesar, agreeing to the politic marriage with Octavia, insisting verbally on his honour, we as well as the Soothsayer note how shabbily he shows there, how inferior in this realm to Caesar—and in more things than cockfights or even guardian geniuses. For Antony is primarily a warrior rather than a politician, and a warrior who affirms rather than denies the sensual life. He cannot live well or heroically in Rome when half his nature is denied. But his decision to return to Egypt does not at all imply an immediate renewal of the heroic Antony; instead, future failure is foreshadowed by the brilliant conjunction of Act II, scene vii and Act III, scene i. In the first scene on Pompey's galley off Misenum we see the drunken revels of the rulers of the world, with Lepidus providing the prophetic image of the man in great place who is not seen to act, Pompey foreshadowing the fate in this realm of *realpolitik* of the man who desires the power possible from dishonourable actions but who refuses the means, and Antony acting out the play's paramount image of the worshipper if not the

incarnation of Bacchus. Antony's loss and the inevitable end of
the decadent triumvirate are suggested by the following scene
in which Ventidius, triumphant against the Parthians in Syria,
refuses to pursue the fleeing enemy for fear that an idle Antony
would resent too great a victory by his own subordinate. In
returning to Egypt Antony initially seems to reject the active
Roman side of his nature as clearly as he tried to reject the sensual Egyptian side when he had left Egypt.

But the shame of the initial and crucial defeat at Actium is
not simply from the Roman point of view: the great Egyptian
lover has publicly shown himself to be a doting mallard. The
itch of his affection has indeed nicked his captainship, but his
failure is of his full humanity:

> My very hairs do mutiny; for the white
> Reprove the brown for rashness, and they them
> For fear, and doting   (III. xi. 13-15)

The failure is anticipated by confusions of sexual roles.[9]
Antony's mindless repetitions of his determination to fight 'By
sea, by sea' despite the pleas of his lieutenants and the anonymous battle-scarred warrior and despite his own experience are
related to Cleopatra's insistence that in the war she will 'appear
there for a man' (III. vii. 18), and Antony's inability in her
presence either to think of her as anything but a woman or to
decide on necessary action. Canidius remarks, 'so our leader's
led, / And we are women's men' (III. vii. 69-70). Enobarbus,
in an aside, states most bluntly the basic objection to Cleopatra's presence in the battle:

> Well, I could reply:
> If we should serve with horse and mares together,
> The horse were merely lost; the mares would bear
> A soldier and his horse.   (6-9)

He spells out the objection more politicly for Cleopatra's ears:

---

[9] Although the notion may be tempting today, I do not believe the play ever suggests an androgynous ideal or even serious use of the tradition of Venus Armata.
Cleopatra and Britomart have little in common: when Cleopatra actually tries to use
military arms, she flees. In their final triumphs both Antony and Cleopatra unite both
Roman and Egyptian values, but they also affirm their own individual roles as man
and woman.

> Your presence needs must puzzle Antony,
> Take from his heart, take from his brain, from's time,
> What should not then be spar'd.   (10-12)

I think that it is precisely such a dazed and subservient Antony whom Cleopatra can betray or abandon in battle, just as it is the termagant, emasculating, and potentially faithless Cleopatra whom Antony can leave or resolve to kill. But when either of the lovers breaks out for a moment from the confines of those roles (roles which the play suggests are sexually unnatural), the other responds, and they again come together.

The ultimate transformations begin just after the defeated Antony's magnificent entrance:

> Hark, the land bids me tread no more upon 't,
> It is asham'd to bear me. Friends, come hither:
> I am so lated in the world that I
> Have lost my way for ever.   (III. xi. 1-4)[10]

He advises his soldiers to abandon him and to seek peace with Caesar. When Cleopatra enters, persuaded by her attendants to approach Antony and to 'comfort him', she is uncertain of her welcome—and she is used to Antony coming running whenever she appears. With wonderful bits of stage business in which ceremony (or its violation) embodies major meanings, the scene builds to emphasize the change in Antony (he does not see Cleopatra, and he does not seem to hear those who tell him that she is there) and the capitulation of Cleopatra to an Antony she no longer rules. She begins with an attempt to follow the old pattern, to make Antony the suitor, but Antony is too deep in memory and soliloquy. At line 45, Cleopatra finally recognizes that she must go to Antony, since he will not come to her; but he still does not immediately respond; when he does, it is not to comfort the queen who Eros says is dying but to ask a devastating question:

> O, whither hast thou led me, Egypt? See,
> How I convey my shame out of thine eyes,
> By looking back what I have left behind
> Stroy'd in dishonour.   (51-4)

For the first time in the play Cleopatra seriously asks forgiveness for something, but her speech is also defensive: 'O my

lord, my lord, / Forgive my fearful sails! I little thought /
You would have follow'd' (54-6). But Antony will not allow her
to escape with a plea of ignorance. He insists on her full knowledge—almost as if the flight of her ships were intended as a
public demonstration of her mastery over him rather than merely
the result of her fear in battle:

> Egypt, thou knew'st too well,
> My heart was to thy rudder tied by the strings,
> And thou shouldst tow me after. O'er my spirit
> Thy full supremacy thou knew'st, and that
> Thy beck might from the bidding of the gods
> Command me.   (56-61)

Cleopatra is reduced to repeated pleas for pardon without ex-
tenuation, 'O, my pardon!' 'Pardon, pardon!' (61, 68), pleas
that, whether sincere or tactical, carry everything before them.
Antony loses his anger:

> Fall not a tear, I say, one of them rates
> All that is won and lost: give me a kiss,
> Even this repays me.   (69-71)

But if Antony has recaptured a degree of his love and can
speak of scorning Fortune, he has not yet recovered his heroic
character. When he tells Cleopatra, 'To the boy Caesar send
this grizzled head, / And he will fill thy wishes to the
brim, / With principalities' (III. xiii. 17-19), she is puzzled by
his tone: 'That head, my lord?' And Antony's ensuing
challenge of Octavius to single combat is, as Enobarbus elo-
quently points out, the pathetically foolish gesture of a
'sworder', one who can imagine that individual physical
powers and skill in fencing might resolve issues which really
require the ability to lead armies and to rule half—or all—of
the world. It is this Antony, I believe, one whom Enobarbus
has almost come to believe it is foolish to serve, whom Cleopatra
can imagine abandoning for a possible new life.

When Caesar's messenger, Thidias, suggests the astonishing
notion that Caesar 'knows that you embrac'd not Antony /
As you did love, but as you fear'd him' (56-7), Cleopatra responds
with a pregnant 'O!' And when Thidias goes on with fairly
crude Roman moralizing ('The scars upon your honour,

therefore, he / Does pity, as constrained blemishes, / Not as deserv'd'—58-60), Cleopatra declares her acquiescence in Caesar's judgement: 'He is a god, and knows / What is most right. Mine honour was not yielded, / But conquer'd merely' (60-2). Enobarbus takes that speech as evidence that Cleopatra has left Antony for Caesar, and it is time for all hands to abandon ship (ll. 62-5). I find nothing in the text to make us question his judgement: the conversation which follows his exit supports it. Cleopatra states her obeisance to Caesar, and when she gives Thidias permission to kiss her hand, her speech implies that the gesture may prove prelude to a revival with the new Caesar of her relationship with the old one (ll. 82-5). Many readers who have attempted to reconcile Cleopatra's apparent betrayal of Antony here with her cursing of herself and Egypt (158-67) and her declaration of love for him shortly afterwards have assumed that Cleopatra must be lying in one place or the other, and therefore look for hints as to her true underlying attitude throughout; but I believe she is as sincere as she can be in both passages. What has changed in the intervening seventy lines or so is Antony. She could well imagine abandoning a pathetic Antony, foolish in defeat; but when Antony comes back a raging lion, one who denounces her with all his passion and with complete independence, who accuses her of not knowing what 'temperance' is but who is really furious that she seems 'cold-hearted' towards him, who above all is 'Antony yet' (93), conscious both of what he is and was and insisting on a relation between the two—for this Antony she has so much love that she would condemn herself and her kingdom to the most dreadful deaths rather than give him up.

It is remarkable how little Cleopatra's magnificent curse has to do with the details of the immediate situation. Here as elsewhere in the last half of the play the characters speak a sort of emotional shorthand, expressing commitments with little concern for the explanations of motives and relationships characteristic of ordinary life. Having received no hint at all of why Cleopatra *had* allowed Thidias to kiss her hand, Antony responds to her passionate speech with a simple 'I am satisfied'. That he is truly so is indicated by his immediate resolve, not to undertake quixotic hand-to-hand combat, but to lead his army against Caesar. Antony has recovered his occupation:

> Dost thou hear, lady?
> If from the field I shall return once more
> To kiss these lips, I will appear in blood,
> I, and my sword, will earn our chronicle:
> There's hope in't yet.
> *Cleopatra.* That's my brave lord!   (172-7)

Antony recovers his martial spirit and his love together. He resolves on one more gaudy night, and Cleopatra responds with a recovery of her own almost lost image:

> It is my birth-day,
> I had thought t' have held it poor. But since my lord
> Is Antony again, I will be Cleopatra.   (185-7)

Enobarbus's response to the scene is, I believe, his one signal (and for him fatal) misinterpretation. But we too may at the moment join in his judgement of Antony's recovery as only foolish valour, particularly when that judgement is followed by Caesar's pity, Antony's pathetic farewell to his followers, and the literally ominous departure 'of the god Hercules'. We are astonished to see in Act IV, scenes iv-viii not a lost Antony but an Antony fully recovered, triumphant both as warrior and lover.

Scene iv begins with Antony's call for his armour. To Cleopatra's 'Sleep a little', he replies simply, 'No, my chuck. Eros! come, mine armour, Eros!' That refusal is Antony's ultimate answer to Pompey's hope that Cleopatra might enchant him so that 'sleep and feeding may prorogue his honour, / Even till a Lethe'd dulness' (II. i. 26-7), and it foreshadows Cleopatra's rejection of Caesar's advice to 'feed, and sleep' (V. ii. 186). As he puts on his armour he becomes before our eyes the renewed image of the heroic Antony which we have heard so much about but have never seen before within the play. Cleopatra tries to help, but she no longer pretends to the masculine knowledge of war: 'Nay, I'll help too. / What's this for?' (IV. iv. 5-6). As she learns, and with Eros continues to arm Antony, she asks, 'Is not this buckled well?' and Antony warmly agrees and even wishes for her presence on the field of battle:

> O love,
> That thou couldst see my wars to-day, and knew'st

> The royal occupation, thou shouldst see
> A workman in't. (15-18)

But she is to stay behind this day; and as he leaves her, there is
no doubt at all either of his affection for her or of his independence and his vocation:

> Fare thee well, dame, whate'er becomes of me:
> This is a soldier's kiss: rebukeable,
> And worthy shameful check it were, to stand
> On more mechanic compliment; I'll leave thee
> Now like a man of steel. (29-33)

At his departure Cleopatra is almost overcome by the double
convictions that if he *could* meet Caesar in single combat this
Antony would win, and that in the immediate military situation his defeat seems inevitable. After the scenes in which
Caesar anticipates his final victory and Enobarbus is struck
with remorse when he receives his treasure, Antony returns
from battle in triumph. Instead of raging that Cleopatra would
allow her hand to be kissed by another, he orders her to give it
to the heroic Scarus, and he addresses her as his sun, the source
of light and energy for his world:

> O thou day o' the world,
> Chain mine arm'd neck, leap thou, attire and all,
> Through proof of harness to my heart, and there
> Ride on the pants triumphing! (IV. viii. 13-16)

Cleopatra responds with full recognition of Antony's achievement, and its rarity and fragility:

> Lord of lords,
> O infinite virtue, com'st thou smiling from
> The world's great snare uncaught?
> (16-18)

As the scene ends with the beginning of a triumphal march,
Antony's voice creates the military music of an almost supernatural Coriolanus—a voice whose tones we will remember
when we hear of his apotheosis within Cleopatra's famous description of her dream in Act V:

> Trumpeters,
> With brazen din blast you the city's ear,
> Make mingle with our rattling tabourines,

That heaven and earth may strike their sounds together,
Applauding our approach.   (IV. viii. 35-9)

That Antony's triumph is to be short-lived is foreshadowed even within these scenes. If in Act IV, scene v we see Antony now determined to fight on land as the old soldier had begged him to do before, we also learn of Enobarbus's desertion; and although we admire Antony's noble generosity to Enobarbus, we anticipate his isolation in 'O, my fortunes have / Corrupted honest men' (16-17). But it is in scene vi that there occurs one of the strangest passages in the drama, one that, I believe, gives us for a moment a totally new perspective on the action and helps to prepare us for the tragedy (and triumph) to come. In Act IV, scenes iv-viii we have been invited to the most nearly complete sympathy with Antony and Cleopatra achieved so far in the play. Octavius Caesar, never viewed very favourably, has been at his most unattractive in III. vi (with his manufacture of political claims and pretended negotiations and his false condolence with Octavia), in III. xii (with his order to Thidias to invent any arguments he can think of to persuade Cleopatra of his friendship), and in IV. i (when he laughingly refuses Antony's challenge and plans to put the deserters in the front ranks against him). Against a revived Antony, he seems to offer no personal heroic qualities whatsoever, only a cold eye for the main chance, an ability to use the rhetoric of honour for his own purposes, efficiency and self-control (without a drop of generosity), an astonishing political sense, and an equally astonishing luck with the cards or the quails. Yet in Act IV, scene vi, after a typically imperial order ('Go forth, Agrippa, and begin the fight: / Our will is Antony be took alive; / Make it so known'), Shakespeare gives him an almost oracular speech, the implications of which go quite beyond Caesar's personal qualities:

> The time of universal peace is near:
> Prove this a prosperous day, the three-nook'd world
> Shall bear the olive freely.   (5-7)[10]

[10] In 'Antony and Cleopatra: "The Time of Universal Peace"', Shakespeare Survey 33 (1980), pp. 99-111, Andrew Fichter comments on the passage and its relation to historical tradition, but I think he pushes too hard for a generally proto-Christian reading. Christian and civic Roman values are the only possible ones he seems to recognize in the play, and he largely ignores the powerful presences of Mars and Venus.

Although his victory is to be delayed one more day, we are firmly reminded for the first time in the play that this unattractive Caesar will be Augustus, the founder of the Pax Romana, and that whatever our personal sympathies, Antony will be (even *must* be) defeated by him.

North's account of how Cleopatra employed Canidius to persuade Antony that she should take a leading part in the war may have suggested to Shakespeare something of the implications and tone of Caesar's speech: 'These fayer perswasions wan him: for it was predestined that the government of all the world should fall into Octavius Caesars handes' (Arden edition, p. 272). But I believe that within their context Shakespeare's lines go beyond the recognition of the fated nature of the Augustan age, for they are followed five lines later by the soliloquy of Enobarbus:

> Alexas did revolt; and went to Jewry on
> Affairs of Antony, there did dissuade
> Great Herod to incline himself to Caesar,
> And leave his master Antony. For this pains,
> Caesar hath hang'd him; Canidius and the rest
> That fell away, have entertainment, but
> No honourable trust: I have done ill,
> Of which I do accuse myself so sorely,
> That I will joy no more.   (12-20)

With details that show Caesar completely untrustworthy, Enobarbus's speech relates 'the time of universal peace' directly to the alliance of Caesar and 'Great Herod of Jewry'.[11] I think it

[11] The earlier appearances of Herod in the play do not at all, I believe, have a similar effect, although in a measure they prepare for and make more startling this one. In Charmian's speech at I. ii. 25-8 ('Let me be married to three kings in a forenoon, and widow them all: let me have a child at fifty, to whom Herod of Jewry may do homage'), Herod seems to be invoked simply as the tyrant whose homage would represent the ultimate feminine conquest—the stock stage figure which some readers see throughout. In III. iii. 2-6, when the messenger is afraid of Cleopatra, Alexas says,

> Good majesty,
> Herod of Jewry dare not look upon you,
> But when you are well pleas'd.
> *Cleopatra.*   That Herod's head
> I'll have: but how, when Antony is gone,
> Through whom I might command it?

The tone of the scene is playfully comic, but there may be a flicker of surprise intended (and achieved) if we remember that Herod will outlive Antony. In III. vi. 73, 'Herod of Jewry' is simply one of the catalogue of kings whom, Caesar tells Octavia, Antony has levied for war; the reference may have added point in that earlier in the scene

doubtful that that juxtaposition could be made anywhere where Christianity was well known without evoking the idea of the Messiah, a figure to whose birth Caesar and Herod are just as indifferent or hostile as they are to Antony and Cleopatra, but to whose predestined mission they unknowingly attend. I do not mean to suggest that *Antony and Cleopatra* suddenly becomes a Christian play; only, that the moment suddenly suggests a new perspective from which we may view the ensuing action with more detachment—as something inevitable and, however painful in part, at some distance from both our ordinary and our most sacred experience. There is also perhaps the hint of an analogy between the sufferings and deaths of these lovers and their apotheosis as timeless Venus and heroic Mars or Hercules, and the birth of the new divinity, the incarnation of a new love which will be proved by suffering in a new world. If it becomes much more than a suggestion, the analogy might undermine the dramatic effectiveness of the last scenes; but the death of Enobarbus, broken-hearted that he has become apostate from the perfect master, and the death of Iras, overcome with compassion as she kisses Cleopatra farewell, may briefly reinforce it.

In the final battle (quickly sketched in twenty-two lines) Antony responds to Caesar's challenge by once again giving the order for sea, although he himself remains with the foot soldiers, ready to fight on land. When he rushes on stage with 'All is lost' he has accepted his defeat as total, and he is convinced that Cleopatra has betrayed him. He seems incapable of imagining defeat as a soldier without defeat or betrayal in love:

> Triple-turn'd whore, 'tis thou
> Hast sold me to this novice, and my heart
> Makes only wars on thee.   (IV. xii. 13-15)

> O this false soul of Egypt! this grave charm,
> Whose eye beck'd forth my wars, and call'd them home;

Caesar had told Maecenas, 'I' the common show-place, where they exercise. / His sons he there proclaim'd the kings of kings . . .' (ll. 12-13). North mentions Herod in the catalogue of kings at the final battle (Arden edition, p. 273), and in relation to Alexas' persuasion (p. 278), but not in close juxtaposition to millennial prophecy. The only phrase I can discover which might have suggested a Christian context to his Elizabethan or Jacobean readers is his reference to 'that contry of Iurie where the true balme is' (p. 268) as one of the provinces which Antony gave to Cleopatra.

Whose bosom was my crownet, my chief end,
Like a right gipsy, hath at fast and loose
Beguil'd me, to the very heart of loss.   (25-9)

When Cleopatra appears and asks, 'Why is my lord enrag'd
against his love?' Antony's manner and language are so violent
that she quickly departs. Alone, he identifies his suffering with
the agonized death of Hercules, and he resolves both on the
death of Cleopatra and on suicide:

The shirt of Nessus is upon me, teach me,
Alcides, thou mine ancestor, thy rage.
Let me lodge Lichas on the horns o' the moon,
And with those hands that grasp'd the heaviest club,
Subdue my worthiest self. The witch shall die,
To the young Roman boy she hath sold me, and I fall
Under this plot: she dies for't.   (xii. 43-9)

When we next see Antony, at the beginning of scene xiv, his
mood has changed remarkably. His conversation with Eros
almost inevitably reminds us of Prospero's most famous speech
in *The Tempest*:

Antony. Eros, thou yet behold'st me?
Eros.   Ay, noble lord.
Antony. Sometime we see a cloud that's dragonish,
A vapour sometime, like a bear, or lion,
A tower'd citadel, a pendent rock,
A forked mountain, or blue promontory
With trees upon 't, that nod unto the world,
And mock our eyes with air. Thou hast seen these
    signs,
They are black vesper's pageants.
Eros.   Ay, my lord.
Antony. That which is now a horse, even with a
    thought
The rack dislimns, and makes it indistinct
As water is in water.
Eros.   It does, my lord.
Antony. My good knave Eros, now thy captain is
Even such a body: here I am Antony,
Yet cannot hold this visible shape, my knave.
I made these wars for Egypt, and the queen,
Whose heart I thought I had, for she had mine:
Which whilst it was mine, had annex'd unto 't

> A million moe, now lost: she, Eros, has
> Pack'd cards with Caesar, and false-play'd my glory
> Unto an enemy's triumph.
> Nay, weep not, gentle Eros, there is left us
> Ourselves to end ourselves.   (1-22)

From that initial question whether Eros *can* still see him, Antony moves beyond a simple recognition of his life as evanescent and dissolving. He seems to conceive of his person as a shape, public as well as private, metaphysical as well as physical—an imprint of a character and a destiny. He is convinced that he has come to the end of his role of action within time and that, function gone, the only way he can affirm the past invisible shape is to end the visible one.

When Mardian comes with the false news of Cleopatra's death, Antony again loses his anger and repents of his suspicions and violence. He has only one desire: to seek death as a reunion with his love. In imagination he is already near her:

> Eros!—I come, my queen:—Eros!—Stay for me,
> Where souls do couch on flowers, we'll hand in hand,
> And with our sprightly port make the ghosts gaze:
> Dido, and her Aeneas, shall want troops,
> And all the haunt be ours.   (50-4)

That Eros loves Antony so much that he would rather die than witness the sorrow of his death adds to our sense of Antony's continually increasing stature. Antony's resolve to be 'A bridegroom in my death, and run into't / As to a lover's bed' results in the mortal agonies that make the suffering of the 'shirt of Nessus' more than a metaphor. His soldiers see the falling of a star and the end of time.

It is remarkable that when Diomedes brings word that Cleopatra is alive, Antony does not utter one word of anger or reproach for the fatal deception. He has accepted his death and he wishes only to be carried to his love. When Cleopatra sees Antony borne by the Guard, she too foresees the end of light and time. The language of the scene is magnificent, but part of the effect is achieved by the symbolic reinforcement of the continuous verbal elevation of the dying Antony by the stage image of Cleopatra and her women drawing up his body from the ground to the tower:

Here's sport indeed! How heavy weighs my lord!
Our strength is all gone into heaviness,
That makes the weight. Had I great Juno's power,
The strong-wing'd Mercury would fetch thee up,
And set thee by Jove's side. Yet come a little,
Wishers were ever fools, O, come, come, come.
            [*They heave Antony aloft to Cleopatra.*
And welcome, welcome! Die when thou hast liv'd,
Quicken with kissing: had my lips that power,
Thus would I wear them out.   (IV. xv. 32-40)

Now the Antony who had wished to kill Cleopatra because he
thought she had sought to make peace with Caesar, and who
had later looked forward to joining her as a bridegroom in
Elysium, advises her to seek from Caesar her honour with her
safety. He cares more for her well-being than for possessing
her, in reality or in dream.

At his death Cleopatra, with wonderfully playful affection,
accuses Antony of being a lover who is not careful enough of
her, and then laments that the world without him has become
too dull to live in:

            Noblest of men, woo't die?
Hast thou no care of me, shall I abide
In this dull world, which in thy absence is
No better than a sty? O, see, my women:
The crown o' the earth doth melt. [*Antony dies.*]
            My Lord?
O wither'd is the garland of the war,
The soldier's pole is fall'n: young boys and girls
Are level now with men: the odds is gone,
And there is nothing left remarkable
Beneath the visiting moon.   (59-68)

When she recovers from her faint, she resolves on an extraordinary blend of Roman style and sexual triumph:

            what's brave, what's noble,
Let's do it after the high Roman fashion,
And make death proud to take us.   (86-8)

In the final scene Cleopatra conceives of her decision as
a choice of permanence, a defeat of the varying fluctuations
of power and emotion in this world. She considers fully the

alternatives: she wishes (and I believe we wish her) to make sure that there is no way by which she can retain both life and nobility. Antony had told her to trust none but Proculeius, but Proculeius betrays her; it is Dolabella whom she moves so by the grandeur of her dream of Antony that he betrays Caesar's intentions to her:

> His legs bestrid the ocean, his rear'd arm
> Crested the world: his voice was propertied
> As all the tuned spheres, and that to friends:
> But when he meant to quail, and shake the orb,
> He was as rattling thunder. For his bounty,
> There was no winter in 't: an autumn 'twas
> That grew the more by reaping: his delights
> Were dolphin-like, they show'd his back above
> The element he lived in: in his livery
> Walk'd crowns and crownets: realms and islands were
> As plates dropp'd from his pocket.   (V. ii. 82-92)

Even if she intends the speech as a tactical manœuvre to gain Dolabella's sympathy, the grand figure possesses Cleopatra's imagination, and it becomes imprinted on our own. Dolabella's answer that there could not be such a man as Cleopatra dreamt of does not at all diminish its force, for Cleopatra insists that Antony was as far beyond the usual creations of fancy as fancy usually goes beyond nature. She recognizes the most significant reality that she has known, and it has become astonishingly enlarged when viewed from the present petty perspective of a world without Antony.

At the end, the ceremonial dressing of Cleopatra as surely restores her image as queen and goddess of love (an image which we have only heard of before, in Enobarbus's description) as Antony's donning of his armour restored his heroic martial image:

> Now, Charmian!
> Show me, my women, like a queen: go fetch
> My best attires. I am again for Cydnus,
> To meet Mark Antony.   (225-8)

As her robe and crown and jewels are placed on her she has 'immortal longings'. She hears Antony call her, praise her noble act, mock Caesar's luck, and she addresses him with a

title she has never used before, implying an ultimate commitment:

> Husband, I come:
> Now to that name, my courage prove my title!   (286-7)

She rushes into death so that Iras will not get Antony's first kiss
in the other world. She dies serenely, addressing the asp as
'poor venomous fool' which would call Caesar 'ass, / Unpoli-
cied' if it could speak; a nurse sucked to sleep by her baby, feeling the approach of death like the bliss of love:

> As sweet as balm, as soft as air, as gentle.
> O Antony! Nay, I will take thee too.
> What should I stay—   (310-12)

And Charmian finishes her mistress's last sentence with 'In
this vile world?' As Charmian closes her mistress's eyes, she
completes the image of a royal goddess:

> Now boast thee, death, in thy possession lies
> A lass unparallel'd. Downy windows, close,
> And golden Phoebus, never be beheld
> Of eyes again so royal! Your crown's awry,
> I'll mend it, and then play.   (314-18)

Charmian's words to the Guard, 'It is well done, and fitting
for a princess / Descended of so many royal kings', are taken
almost verbatim from North, but they may remind us how
carefully Shakespeare selected what he wanted from that
source. In North the royal robes and crown are placed on a Cleopatra who, before her meeting with Caesar, had pulled out her
hair, scratched her face and stomach, and blubbered her eyes
in her mourning for Antony.[12] North's image has its own
pathos, but it is utterly incongruent with Shakespeare's
transcendent image of beauty and nobility.

I do not believe we are much concerned with most of the words
of Caesar and his soldiers at the end; they, or something like
them, are necessary chiefly so that we can have sufficient time
to contemplate the royal figure. Three of Caesar's responses
are, however, crucial for the effect of the scene, and they are all

[12] See Arden edition, p. 283.

the more impressive because the cold Caesar makes them:

> Bravest at the last,
> She levell'd at our purposes, and being royal
> Took her own way. . . .   (333-5)

>   . . . she looks like sleep,
> As she would catch another Antony
> In her strong toil of grace.   (344-6)

> She shall be buried by her Antony.
> No grave upon the earth shall clip in it
> A pair so famous: high events as these
> Strike those that make them: and their story is
> No less in pity than his glory which
> Brought them to be lamented. Our army shall
> In solemn show attend this funeral,
> And then to Rome. Come, Dolabella, see
> High order, in this great solemnity. (356-64)

The very last lines seem to refer to much more than the funeral rites which are to follow. We have watched the passionate and disorderly history of Antony and Cleopatra as it was transformed into a 'great solemnity' of love, and we have sensed in its final moments a state and an 'order' both 'high' and mysterious.

VII

The Anger of Prospero:
The Tempest

The Tempest may well be both the most loved play of Shakespeare and the one that most readers have the hardest time talking about convincingly. (I have found Northrop Frye and Reuben Brower the two chief exceptions to the latter generalization.)[1] It concerns all the great themes: the stage, magic, art and nature, mercy and vengeance, reconciliation, the procession of the generations, the masque of the elements. Someone has remarked that most readers of English agree about *The Tempest*'s greatness because it can be read so as to fit any conceivable allegorical system that is imposed upon it. Everyone agrees that the play says something significant about human life, but it is difficult for anyone to convince others of *what* he thinks it says.

With most Shakespeare plays I think it usually proves more fruitful to begin with dramatic problems instead of messages. I believe most readers and hearers of *The Tempest* have probably had some difficulties with Act I, scene ii, that scene of over 500 lines which sets the stage for what is to follow. It is the scene in which we are given a great deal of information and in which we are introduced to Prospero, Miranda, Ariel, and Caliban—and even to Ferdinand as a recognizable character. After Ariel leads Ferdinand on stage at line 376,[2] the scene ends strongly. The chief problems are with the first 186-line conversation between Prospero and Miranda. Although few critics have paid much attention to the scene as a whole, I believe the usual

---

[1] Frye has written frequently about *The Tempest*, which is central to his concerns with romance; one of his most condensed, and at the same time comprehensive, considerations is in the preface to his Pelican edition of the play (Penguin Books, 1959 and 1970). Brower's essay, 'The Mirror of Analogy: "The Tempest"', appeared in *The Fields of Light: An Experiment in Critical Reading* (New York, 1951), pp. 95-122.

[2] Frank Kermode's New Arden edition first appeared in 1954. I quote throughout from the corrected 6th edition (Cambridge, Mass., 1961).

attitude is a tolerant understanding of Shakespeare's 'problem' in having to pack in so much information at the beginning if the rest of the play is to sustain so beautifully the unity (almost the identity) of time. Sometimes I think I have detected a certain pleasure on the critic's part that it is so easy for him to detect the seams and flaws in the great master's final work. (That the structure of the rest of the play is so miraculous seldom seems to suggest to these commentators the twinges of self-doubt one might justifiably expect.) A number of readers seem to assume that Shakespeare is as eager to get on to the messages and the symbols as they are, and that he has therefore written the scene casually, in a deliberately slapdash manner.

While critics and scholars are free to ignore what fails to arouse their interest, directors and actors have to get through all the scenes and speeches and must therefore both try to understand them and to make them interesting to their audiences. Their efforts with this scene have sometimes been almost desperate. A number of Shakespeare productions seem to have been conceived with the assumption that Shakespeare is an old-fashioned bore who could hardly be expected to command the interest of sophisticated moderns without strenuous efforts to bring him up to date. In this scene as in other Shakespearian scenes in which actors may find speeches too long or dull, players often try to dramatize them by extravagant changes of tone and pace and by arbitrary pauses. I have only once heard the lines of this scene read in a public theatre as both intelligible and rapidly moving verse.[3]

That experience helped convince me that the scene is successful, that decent actors can play it so as to hold the interest of almost any audience if they understand what is going on in it. Not simply an attempt to sketch the background for the play, it is part of the play. In addition to introducing us to Prospero and to his relations with four of the most important characters, the scene also, by revealing Prospero's past history and his

---

[3] The occasion was a performance of the touring Prospect Theatre Company in Belfast during the autumn of 1966. Timothy West was the finest Prospero I have seen, and the other actors were good. Although there were numbers of noisy children in the audience, the production worked beautifully despite dusty costumes, sketchy scenery, and a dowdy masque: the actors knew how to move and to speak and they seemed to understand their lines.

plans for the future, dramatizes the importance (and the pressure) of these few dramatic moments of time. In his plays Shakespeare characteristically makes the first appearance of his major characters decisive for their later development. Whatever happens to the characters and however much they may change, the happenings and the changes are related to or consonant with the initial appearances. Significances and resemblances and analogues may multiply and expand, particularly in the later plays, but we are not free to make identities or direct equivalences which are incongruent with or contradicted by the major initial scenes. This first scene in which we see and hear Prospero provides not only some directions for our imagination, but also some limitations on what we are free to make of Prospero and his role and his language within the rest of the play.

In the extraordinary opening scene of the play we have seen and heard a wild tempest in which a ship breaks up with all hands on board. Only the tone of Gonzalo's speeches, particularly the last one,[4] makes us doubt our proper sympathetic response to catastrophe. In scene ii Miranda, who has seen what we have seen and heard the cries (but not the dialogue), expresses directly her compassion and her lament for the loss of any life as well as her wish for the power to have prevented the loss. But we, like Miranda, learn from Prospero that this is a realm in which we literally cannot believe our eyes and our ears: 'There's no harm done' (15). What we see happen may not truly have happened; what we hear may not be true. On this island we are left in more than the usual uncertainties:

> No, not so much perdition as an hair
> Betid to any creature in the vessel
> Which thou heard'st cry, which thou saw'st sink.
> (30-2)

For the explanation of such phenomena, an explanation that the audience needs quite as much as Miranda, Prospero ceremoniously divests himself of his magic garment—his extraordinary power, his special status and authority in his roles of magus, teacher, and even father: 'Lie there, my Art' (24). If we have

---

4 'Now would I give a thousand furlongs of sea for an acre of barren ground, long heath, broom, furze, anything. The wills above be done! but I would fain die a dry death' (I. i. 64-7).

been deluded in the first scene into identifying as a violent con-
vulsion of nature what is really the evidence of one man's preternatural powers, we obviously need to see him without those
powers to get any notion of his true nature. But Prospero's taking off his mantle immediately dramatizes also that he is to give
his fifteen-year-old daughter the knowledge (and therefore the
freedom) which will enable her to judge him—his past actions
and present plans as a ruler and a brother as well as a father.
He has often before started to tell her the history of their lives,
but has put off the revelation with 'Stay: not yet' (36). It cannot be put off any longer: 'The hour's now come; / The very
minute bids thee ope thine ear; / Obey, and be attentive.' The
last instruction is particularly interesting. At the very moment
when he is to give Miranda the information that will make her
no longer totally dependent on him for judgement and action,
he orders her to obey. Prospero, like most fathers standing
before their children awaiting judgement, feels anxious, vulnerable, tempted to assert his authority. He is testy, on the
edge of anger.

Of course the situation provides tests of Miranda's as well as
Prospero's humanity. Miranda, truly a wonder, rises to all the
challenges of the scene—as of the rest of the play—marvellously. Her initial response to the news that her father was the
rightful Duke of Milan and she 'his only heir / And princess'
(58-9) is not to lament the loss (and therefore to imply a pejorative judgement on her education and the life they have led on
the island), but simply to ask the alternative questions, 'What
foul play had we, that we came from thence? / Or blessed
was't we did?' (60-1). But Prospero finds it impossible to feel
assured in advance of her sympathetic response to the details of
his failure as a Duke and his brother's betrayal. He punctuates
his narrative with a series of phrases demanding Miranda's
attention and, implicitly, her sympathy:

> I pray thee, mark me, that a brother should
> Be so perfidious!   (67-8)
>
>   Thy false uncle—
> Dost thou attend me?   (77-8)
>
> Thou attend'st not?   (87)

> hence his ambition growing,—
> Dost thou hear?   (105-6)

> Mark his condition, and th'event; then tell me
> If this might be a brother.   (117-18)

> Hear a little further,
> And then I'll bring thee to the present business
> Which now's upon 's . . .   (135-7)

Almost every imperative or question is like a physical shake: not merely 'Do you *hear* me?' but, as often with that phrase, 'Are you listening with sympathy? Are you *with* me?'

Prospero has reason to be a nervous narrator. Despite all his special pleading, his story indicates that he had thoughtlessly made Lear's crucial mistake of assuming that one can retain the title and power of a ruler while neglecting or abandoning the functions and duties. Prospero's claim that his own virtues begat evils in his brother is surely seriously flawed:

> my trust,
> Like a good parent, did beget of him
> A falsehood in its contrary, as great
> As my trust was; which had indeed no limit,
> A confidence sans bound.   (93-7)

No parent, at least by Shakespearian standards, is supposed to have a trust in his child so boundless that he reverses the natural roles of parent and child, and that is precisely the analogy to what Prospero did in the political realm: he made Antonio the Duke's ruler. But Miranda does not respond in judgement to any of this; she is moved to mild reprimand only in response to her father's claim that Antonio cannot truly be his brother:

> I should sin
> To think but nobly of my grandmother:
> Good wombs have borne bad sons.
>   (118-20)

Her only other comments are to lament the trouble she was to Prospero when he was exiled and to express a wish to see the good Gonzalo. Surely the warmth of Prospero's response ('O, a cherubin / Thou wast that did preserve me'—152-3) is related to her present sympathy as well as to the memory of her infant smiles.

After Prospero arises (and presumably resumes his magic cloak), Miranda has a question:

> And now, I pray you, sir,
> For still 'tis beating in my mind, your reason
> For raising this sea-storm?   (175-7)

Prospero's answer leads both into the rest of the scene and into the action of the entire play:

> Know thus far forth.
> By accident most strange, bountiful Fortune,
> (Now my dear lady) hath mine enemies
> Brought to this shore; and by my prescience
> I find my zenith doth depend upon
> A most auspicious star, whose influence
> If now I court not, but omit, my fortunes
> Will ever after droop.   (177-84)

With limited prescience, Prospero is to have for a few hours something like the power of providence to work out a happy ending. The situation is like the fairy stories in which the central character is granted his wish for power with a limit—for one or three deeds or until the clock strikes midnight. In a tragic context such power results in general and self-destruction, and the pressure of time, the limited moments in which the actions must occur, becomes, as for Brutus and Macbeth, a nightmare.[5] In comedy the pressure of time makes for tension and laughter. The inventions are often pleasing or interesting in themselves (disguises, illusions, mazes, bed-tricks, frozen swords and boiled brains), but Prospero and the Duke of *Measure for Measure* also risk a certain loss of dignity, become occasionally the objects rather than the directors of our laughter as their quick improvisations and busy interventions show them on the verge of being the creatures rather than the masters of their creations. If Prospero and the other Duke are ever truly figures of divine providence, it is only as they provide comically flawed human imitations of the extraordinary lengths to which God must go in order to grant human beings freedom while still keeping them from destroying themselves. Stage comedy

---

[5] Cf. *Julius Caesar*, II. i. 61-9 and *Macbeth*, II. I. 33-64.

insists that we recognize the distance between the human imitator and the divine model.

But if Prospero is sometimes unconsciously comic, he also, with the possible exception of Lear, shows the shortest temper of any admirable character in Shakespeare. Part of the irascibility stems from the same source as much of the comedy: the anxiety of a human being who is nervously attempting a providential role for a few, decisive hours. (Prospero's anger itself can sometimes seem comic to us if not to him.) But as the first part of the second scene clearly indicates, a good deal of Prospero's temper is related directly to the special circumstances of this comedy, in which the leading role is given to a father instead of to the lovers. His role invites judgement not only for his past but also for the present and future. He must work to regain his power so that he may pass it on to the generation which is immediately reaching maturity. There is surely some tension or anxiety about even the most complete fulfilment of his plans: his dream of a happy ending will involve giving up his daughter in marriage rather than acquiring a bride; his desired future role is a strictly temporary one as Duke of Milan, 'where / Every third thought shall be' his 'grave' (V. i. 310-11).

Later in the second scene the simple anxiety expressed in testy questions and attention-demanding imperatives to Miranda changes to open anger with Ariel and Caliban. When Ariel reminds Prospero of his promise of liberty, Prospero's tone is sharp:

> Before the time be out? no more!   (246)
> Thou liest, malignant thing!   (257)

He is placated only when Ariel expresses gratitude for past deliverance, asks pardon, and promises to perform the immediate tasks. Prospero's anger with Caliban is more constant and more intemperately expressed:

> Thou poisonous slave, got by the devil himself
> Upon thy wicked dam, come forth!   (321-2)

> Thou most lying slave,
> Whom stripes may move, not kindness! I have us'd thee,
> Filth as thou art, with human care . . .   (346-8)

As the quotations indicate, Prospero's anger towards Caliban varies from that of one injured by incarnate evil to that of a thoroughly exasperated teacher with a recalcitrant student on whom pedagogy is quite wasted; it is difficult to be sure which attitude is responsible for the greater violence of expression. The violence and the general context of his speeches might suggest that Prospero's description of Caliban's paternity shows more about Prospero's emotion than about the facts in the case. (The tone of the speeches, coupled with the fact that Miranda never shows any anger elsewhere in the play, would seem the chief argument in favour of Theobald's ascription of lines 353-64 to Prospero.)[6]

At the end of the scene, Prospero's asides ('but this swift business / I must uneasy make, lest too light winning / Make the prize light'—453-5) assure us that his immediate anger towards Ferdinand and Miranda is simulated. It is, however, dramatically convincing as he plays the role of heavy father and threatened ruler:

> A word, good sir;
> I fear you have done yourself some wrong: a word.
>   (445-6)

> Follow me.
> Speak not you for him: he's a traitor. Come;
> I'll manacle thy neck and feet together:
> Sea-water shalt thou drink; thy food shall be
> The fresh-brook mussels, wither'd roots, and husks
> Wherein the acorn cradled. Follow.   (462-7)

> What! I say,
> My foot my tutor?   (471-2)

---

[6] Kermode notes (New Arden edition, p. 32) that Theobald 'followed Dryden's guess', but he rejects assigning the lines to Prospero on the grounds that 'none of the many editors has succeeded in justifying this interference'. Kermode's most telling argument for Miranda as the speaker may be that 'In 365-7 Caliban is addressing both father and daughter (he calls Prospero *thou* throughout) when he speaks of being taught language'. But doesn't Caliban address Prospero as *you* in 344-6: 'and here you sty me / In this hard rock, whiles you do keep from me / The rest o' th' island'? Kermode seems to argue for an authorial consistency in the uses of *thou* and *you* similar to the realistic or psychological consistency which he summarily dismisses in the arguments for Miranda as speaker: 'None of this seems to take into account Shakespeare's habitual disregard of this kind of immediate probability.'

> Silence! one word more
> Shall make me chide thee, if not hate thee. What!
> An advocate for an impostor! hush!   (478-80)

At the end of the scene it is good to be reassured by Miranda that Prospero's behaviour (and language) so far are not at all characteristic:

> Be of comfort;
> My father's of a better nature, sir,
> Than he appears by speech: this is unwonted
> Which now came from him.   (498-501)

Later in Act IV, in response to Prospero's most violent and most significant outburst of anger, Miranda remarks to Ferdinand:

> Never till this day
> Saw I him touch'd with anger, so distemper'd.
> (IV. i. 144-5)

Irascibility could hardly be the natural temperament of the good father, the white magician, the man who will be a just and temperate ruler. The contrast between a good man's extraordinary anger and the habitual behaviour of villains has already been anticipated in the brief first scene of the play. There, the Boatswain is trying to save the ship. When he is interrupted by a hierarchical procession of ordinary political powers, he first 'prays' them to keep below—get out of the way. With a question from Antonio, the request quickly modulates to a command. When Gonzalo, shocked at impropriety and concerned with ordinary protocol, replies, 'Nay, good, be patient' (15), the Boatswain's justified impatience turns to open anger:

> When the sea is. Hence! What cares these roarers for the name of King? To cabin: silence! trouble us not.   (16-18)

The Boatswain instinctively believes that in a tempest the true king is the man who can save the ship and the lives on board.[7] It is a work that requires extraordinary skills, energy, and

---

[7] In 'Marvell's "lusty Mate" and the Ship of the Commonwealth', *Modern Language Notes*, 76 (1961), 106-10, John Wallace comments on the history and the later political development of the traditional figure.

alertness at every moment. And while the Boatswain shows impatient anger with those who interfere with the work that must be done, he devotes his chief energy to the work itself and to encouraging those who will aid in it: 'Cheerly, good hearts!' to his fellow sailors comes directly before his 'Out of our way, I say' to the landlubber nobility. The Boatswain is even annoyed by the distracting cries of those who fear drowning. But his generalized 'A plague upon this howling!' is directly contrasted with the specific curses of Sebastian and Antonio, for whom surliness and anger are natural modes:

Sebastian. A pox o' your throat, you bawling, blasphemous incharitable dog!
Boatswain. Work you, then.
Antonio. Hang, cur! hang, you whoreson, insolent noisemaker.

(40-4)

Antonio's and Sebastian's response to the immediate possibility of sudden death is remarkably incommensurate with the occasion; it resembles Goneril's reaction to Edmund's mortal wound:[8] the entire situation is annoying and, besides, unfair:

> *Sebastian.*   I'm out of patience.
> *Antonio.* We are merely cheated of our lives by drunkards . . .

(54-5)

Although Prospero's (and the Boatswain's) kind of anger is clearly distinguished from that of the villains, it is also surely one of the faults which, as his Epilogue suggests, bind him to humanity both on the island and in the audience.

Antonio and Sebastian may be moved to anger by the Boatswain and the storm and to annoyance by Gonzalo's loquacity, but when they come to planning and attempting murder they seem not to be possessed by any emotion so serious, only by rather trivial, mildly stirring desires for power and status. It is Caliban who has mastered the most full-mouthed curses of the play for his master, his usurper, his tormentor:

> As wicked dew as e'er my mother brush'd
> With raven's feather from unwholesome fen

8
　　　　　　　This is practice, Gloucester;
　　By th' law of war thou wast not bound to answer
　　An unknown opposite; thou art not vanquish'd,
　　But cozen'd and beguil'd.
　　　　　　　　　　　　(*King Lear*. V. iii. 151-4.)

> Drop on you both! a south-west blow on ye
> And blister you all o'er!   (I. ii. 323-6)

> All the charms
> Of Sycorax, toads, beetles, bats, light on you!
>   (341-2)

> You taught me language; and my profit on't
> Is, I know how to curse. The red plague rid you
> For learning me your language!   (365-7)

He is truly the son of Sycorax, who 'in her most unmitigable rage' had confined Ariel 'Into a cloven pine' for refusing 'To act her earthy and abhorr'd commands' (272-7). Caliban's hatred and anger are so intense that, as in his initial meeting with Trinculo and Stephano, we do not know how many of the torments he ascribes to Prospero are merely his own interpretations of accidents and chance. In the first scene with the clowns, Caliban's violence is subordinated to the comedy of his discovery of sack and a new god and his notion of freedom. But there is nothing comic in his imagined murdering of Prospero, where his words are surrogates for physical actions:

> I'll yield him thee asleep,
> Where thou mayst knock a nail into his head.
>   (III. ii. 59-60)

> Why, as I told thee, 'tis a custom with him
> I'th'afternoon to sleep; there thou mayst brain him,
> Having first seiz'd his books; or with a log
> Batter his skull, or paunch him with a stake,
> Or cut his wezand with thy knife.   (III. ii. 85-9)

Shakespeare takes extraordinary risks here and elsewhere in the play. The final speech is *possible* in a comedy only because it is preceded by Ariel's ventriloquist manipulation of the trio and by their comic (and harmless) anger and brawling, and because it is followed by Caliban's imaginative description of a dream of harmony and paradise, a speech so moving that it guarantees that Caliban cannot be dismissed at the end of the play as merely evil or stupid:

> Be not afeard; the isle is full of noises,
> Sounds and sweet airs, that give delight, and hurt not.
> Sometimes a thousand twangling instruments

> Will hum about mine ears; and sometime voices,
> That, if I then had wak'd after long sleep,
> Will make me sleep again: and then, in dreaming,
> The clouds methought would open, and show riches
> Ready to drop upon me; that, when I wak'd,
> I cried to dream again.   (III. ii. 133-41)

But a number of Caliban's speeches are the purest expression of mortal anger uncontaminated by other human motives. It is an anger at the farthest remove from the testiness of Prospero with Miranda, the Boatswain's anger with those who interfere with the ship, Prospero's anger at an Ariel who wishes to quit his labour, or the comic anger of Stephano and Trinculo. It is much closer to the desperate anger turned against the self which Ariel describes in Prospero's masque of judgement of Alonso, Sebastian, and Antonio:

> You are three men of sin . . .
>
>   I have made you mad;
> And even with such-like valour men hang and drown
> Their proper selves.   (III. iii. 53-60)

That anger, too, is given a context which makes it possible within comedy. The judgement is ritualistic and purgative. Ariel pronounces that 'heart-sorrow / And a clear life ensuing', the traditional proofs of true repentance, will prevent the fulfilment of the curse. And once again the drawn swords frozen in the air are a sign not merely that one cannot fight spirits with physical violence, but also that preternatural power is present, determined to prevent violence and death and tragedy no matter how intent some of the human participants are on all three.

Assured that 'these mine enemies are all knit up / In their distractions: they now are in my power' (III. iii. 89-90), Prospero returns to Ferdinand and Miranda. In an almost Jamesian manner, Shakespeare avoids the big scene of Prospero's discovery of his true motives to the lovers and his agreement to their betrothal—after all, we pretty well know what *must* have happened.[9] Instead, the imaginative camera focuses only on

---

[9] One is reminded of the omission of the expected big recognition scene in *The Winter's Tale*; in that case, however, in anticipation of the final 'statue scene', Shakespeare developed at length the spectators' response of astonishment and wonder.

the end of the scene and on Prospero's gift of the masque—a beautiful work of art, a wish for all the best in a fruitful, paradisal state more ordered and sustained than Caliban's dream, a spectacle which will give the couple something to occupy their minds besides dalliance. After the initial invitation of Iris, Ceres responds. Iris assures her that the childish Cupid and the intemperate Venus have been defeated, and Juno and Ceres celebrate the coming wedding with their song of blessing:

> Juno. *Honour, riches, marriage-blessing,*
> *Long continuance, and increasing,*
> *Hourly joys be still upon you!*
> *Juno sings her blessings on you.*
> Ceres. *Earth's increase, foison plenty,*
> *Barns and garners never empty;*
> *Vines with clust'ring bunches growing;*
> *Plants with goodly burthen bowing;*
> *Spring come to you at the farthest*
> *In the very end of harvest!*
> *Scarcity and want shall shun you;*
> *Ceres' blessing so is on you.*
>   (IV. i. 106-17)

It is no wonder that Ferdinand is so charmed that for the moment he wishes to remain on the island forever—however problematic a prince's and husband's future might be on an island with only his wife and an all-powerful father-in-law. Iris calls the Nymphs and Reapers to perform a dance. It is towards the end of the dance, that artful, measured image of beauty and a life at one with nature, that a stage direction describes the dissolution of the vision—and implies the limitation of the fiction:

Enter certain Reapers, properly habited: they join with the Nymphs in a graceful dance; towards the end whereof PROSPERO starts suddenly, and speaks; after which, to a strange, hollow, and confused noise, they heavily vanish.

The text gives Prospero's aside and his interrupting words after the description:

> I had forgot that foul conspiracy
> Of the beast Caliban and his confederates
> Against my life: the minute of their plot
> Is almost come. [*To the Spirits.*] Well done! avoid; no more!
>   (139-42)

Frank Kermode makes a strange remark about the passage: 'The apparently unnecessary perturbation of Prospero at the thought of Caliban may be a point at which an oddly pedantic concern for classical structure causes it to force its way through the surface of the play' (Arden edition, p. lxxv). But surely Prospero's anger *is* 'necessary' here—and for reasons not at all pedantic. Here, more economically than elsewhere in the play, a movement images meanings crucial to the drama: a sudden intervention to prevent threatened violence, the necessary breaking of an idealized artful form, the blasting of a dream of perfection by the threat of evil, the interruption of contemplation by the necessity of action. It is a movement basic to the action of *The Tempest*—the fate and dream of Prospero. And although occasionally the business of the human imitator of providence (accompanied by our comfortable assurance that all will turn out for the best in the world of comedy) may invite us to smile at the protagonist, such a response is not evoked here. For we, like Prospero, had for the moment become so engrossed in a vision of beauty and a world of love without winter that we too had forgotten the immediate threat of evil and the necessity of action if any sort of happiness is to be achieved—and we resent the reminder.[10] If Prospero is a father angered that he cannot even give his daughter an unflawed betrothal present because of the demands of reality, we are those whose expectations of formal perfection in the masque and dance have been rudely broken. We can sympathize with the anger of Prospero. It is only the lovers, those who could imagine an entire future of masque productions on the island and who know nothing whatsoever of the immediate threats of evil and disorder, who are totally perplexed. It is to his newly prospective son-in-law, in an attempt to explain the 'passion / That works' him so

---

[10] The effect recalls the forgetfulness of the audience in the last Act of *King Lear* ('Great thing of us forgot!'); at both moments, reminded of our own failures of attention or purpose, we react with guilt or resentment or surprise which involves us directly in the responses of the dramatic participants. At such moments Shakespeare allows no one in the theatre to feel invulnerable or superior. One reader has suggested a non-Shakespearian analogy in Act IV, scene iv of *The Alchemist*, when the clerk Dapper calls off-stage and both Face and the audience have forgotten his existence in the eleven scenes of complex intrigue that have intervened since he was bestowed in the privy at the end of Act III.

strongly, that Prospero addresses the most famous speech in the play:

> You do look, my son, in a mov'd sort,
> As if you were dismay'd: be cheerful, sir.
> Our revels now are ended. These our actors,
> As I foretold you, were all spirits, and
> Are melted into air, into thin air:
> And, like the baseless fabric of this vision,
> The cloud-capp'd towers, the gorgeous palaces,
> The solemn temples, the great globe itself,
> Yea, all which it inherit, shall dissolve,
> And, like this insubstantial pageant faded,
> Leave not a rack behind. We are such stuff
> As dreams are made on; and our little life
> Is rounded with a sleep. Sir, I am vex'd;
> Bear with my weakness; my old brain is troubled:
> Be not disturb'd with my infirmity:
> If you be pleas'd, retire into my cell,
> And there repose: a turn or two I'll walk,
> To still my beating mind.   (IV. i. 146-63)

There seems little more reason why this marvellous speech should be taken out of its context and considered the ultimate message of the play or the true voice of the private non-dramatic Shakespeare than that Macbeth's judgement that life 'is a tale / Told by an idiot, full of sound and fury, / Signifying nothing'[11] should be thought the burden of that drama. Macbeth's statement is that of a military hero who has committed spiritual suicide and who can imagine no safety while any other human being lives and has power: it is certainly true for him at that moment in the play. Similarly, Prospero's is the speech of a particular character at a particular moment in the drama: a masque presenter whose performance is interrupted, a magician who is becoming tired of the necessity of magic, a disappointed father, a former Duke who must return with some reluctance to the duties of ruling, a man of imagination who is weary of action and can imagine the end even of dreams like Caliban's of the sounds of blessing. And the speech is tied firmly to its immediate dramatic context: Ferdinand should not be dismayed either by the ending of the revels or by Prospero's

---

11 *Macbeth*, V. v. 26-8.

anger, nor should he be haunted by Prospero's analogous vision of the insubstantiality of all human creations and even human life—the response of an old man, vexed, infirm, with a beating mind, needing rest. Prospero, like most of Shakespeare's admirable characters, is not concerned with trying to impose a 'mature' point of view on young lovers; instead, he apologizes for intruding such an inappropriate vision upon their happiness. They, not at all comprehending, answer him with a charity and a unity that bode well for their future: 'We wish your peace' (163).

The restoration of Prospero's peace is not immediate. Despite his forgetfulness, the more-or-less disembodied Ariel has not allowed the low characters' plot for murder and subversion to proceed. Prospero is still angry at the thought of Caliban:

> A devil, a born devil, on whose nature
> Nurture can never stick; on whom my pains,
> Humanely taken, all, all lost, quite lost;
> And as with age his body uglier grows,
> So his mind cankers. I will plague them all,
> Even to roaring.   (IV. i. 188-93)

And he does. The anger of the teacher or the creator can be a dangerous thing:

> Fury, Fury! there, Tyrant, there! hark, hark!
> Go charge my goblins that they grind their joints
> With dry convulsions; shorten up their sinews
> With aged cramps; and more pinch-spotted make them
> Than pard or cat o' mountain.   (257-61)

At this moment Prospero achieves the position which some people have imagined as the chief constituent of a happy ending: 'At this hour / Lies at my mercy all mine enemies' (262-3).

Everyone knows the resolution: Ariel's imaginative sympathy for the maze-struck nobility and Prospero's determination to be fully human in his sympathies:

> Though with their high wrongs I am struck to th' quick,
> Yet with my nobler reason 'gainst my fury
> Do I take part: the rarer action is
> In virtue than in vengeance: they being penitent,

> The sole drift of my purpose doth extend
> Not a frown further. Go release them, Ariel:
> My charms I'll break, their senses I'll restore,
> And they shall be themselves.   (V. i. 24-32)

It is a moving speech and, within the full context of the play, almost an inevitable one. The play obviously concerns reconciliation and forgiveness, and certainly no one within the Christian tradition could question the righteous determination to forgive the penitent. But there are some problems. It is never clear that, despite their torments, the chief villains are at all penitent. Since the play suggests that only the good can perceive the good, one might take Sebastian's exclamation at the sight of Ferdinand and Miranda, 'A most high miracle!' (177), as evidence that he has experienced something like penitence and that his future actions might even show it. But so far as I can tell, there is no single word from Antonio that indicates he regrets anything, no indication that the self to which he is restored is anything but a fairly sorry one. It is an important point, I believe, and I think it indicates both that Prospero's decision is a truly remarkable one and that Shakespeare is a good deal more realistic than some of his commentators. It should be easy enough for a good man to forgive a true penitent (as Prospero forgives Gonzalo and even Alonso), or for a powerful man to abandon extraordinary power if he believed he had helped create a truly 'redeemed society' in which evil was finally eliminated. But Prospero's decision to forgive the villains, or at least not to hang them for treason or otherwise punish them, is more difficult and more significant than either of these. Prospero has not redeemed the world; his miracle is much smaller than that. All he has done is to make good an old wrong (for which he is largely responsible), and to provide a chance for another generation to make a new beginning—with the evil still present and his only defence against its future occurrences some detailed knowledge that he can use as benevolent blackmail. Although his language may indicate that he does not fully understand the implications himself, Prospero's decision to abjure his 'rough magic' is a decision to leave the realm of the demigods and rejoin the human race, to allow ordinary, fallible human life and society to continue, with no guarantee at all of an ultimate and *final* happy ending, only the hope that, with succeeding generations, a number of happy endings (or, more properly, new beginnings) may be momentarily achieved. If we are to allow a comic vision, one that celebrates love and marriage and a new generation's assumption of power, we must, if not absolutely love our enemies, at least allow them to live. The alternative to Prospero's choice, for drama or for politics or for the family, would be a frozen state which would require revolution rather than reconciliation if life, with its succession of the generations, were to continue.

Prospero's last truly magical command (after all, the audience's applause must fill the sails for Naples) is for the heavenly music which dissolves the charms and allows every man to find himself 'when no man was his own' (V. i. 212-13). There are two scenes of formal reconciliation with the noblemen, both wonderfully effective on the stage. At the beginning of the first one, Alonso, Gonzalo, Sebastian, Antonio, Adrian, and Francisco stand, still unconscious, in a charmed circle; their frozen 'frantic' gestures of the tormented only gradually relax as Prospero pronounces his private judgement on them before they consciously hear his words. Like the interrupted masque and Prospero's anger in Act IV, the scene images the sort of significances that it is usually difficult enough even to describe: purgation, overcoming the demands for justice, the dissolution of 'ignorant fumes' with the coming of the sun and the return of the tide of reason to the mudflats of delusion and insanity. Prospero's speech makes clear the differing measures and meanings of his 'forgiveness'. His love for 'Holy Gonzalo' is unlimited, but his private condemnation of evil increases as he turns from Alonso, to Sebastian, and to Antonio. The lack of cloudy sentiment in his remark to Antonio, 'I do forgive thee, / Unnatural though thou art' (78-9), clearly anticipates the later formal (and comic) public judgement:

> For you, most wicked sir, whom to call brother
> Would even infect my mouth, I do forgive
> Thy rankest fault,—all of them; and require
> My dukedom of thee, which perforce, I know,
> Thou must restore.   (130-4)

That Prospero considers Antonio's faults so many and so 'rank' that he could not possibly decide on one as the rankest suggests clearly enough how conditional is his forgiveness, how little he assumes Antonio's repentance, how little he truly welcomes him into the re-established dukedom. But aside from that one speech, Prospero's public stance with the nobles is that of the man who forgives and heals, the reconciler, the gracious host who welcomes his guests to the island. He must continually reassure Gonzalo and Alonso of the reality both of their present experience and of his own forgiveness. To achieve those ends, his embraces are probably more important than his language. His 'miracle' of the discovery of the young lovers playing chess is made partly as recompense to Alonso for the restoration of the dukedom, but also directly in reply to Alonso's lament for the loss of Ferdinand:

> Irreparable is the loss; and patience
> Says it is past her cure. (V. i. 140-1)

Prospero, who had had so little patience in the time of immediate crisis, possesses it fully and playfully when the crucial moral action is completed and the end of the voyage in sight. And the vision is of lost lovers playing a game in which neither 'playing false' nor 'wrangling' at all disturbs love or patience—a vision which causes Sebastian to concede a miracle and which results in Ferdinand's regret for his former cursing of the merciful seas, and Alonso's blessing of Ferdinand and Miranda. The vision marks the transformation of sorrow and impatience to wonder and joy at the beauty and bravery of mankind and the world:

> O, wonder!
> Hom many goodly creatures are there here!
> How beauteous mankind is! O brave new world,
> That has such people in 't!   (181-4)

Prospero's ''Tis new to thee', states succinctly a major theme of the play: that to a large degree we perceive the world in terms of what we are. At this moment he does not at all openly question the goodness of these chastened couriers, usurpers, and would-be murderers; he only insists that they represent the same world that he (and we) have known before.

Continually in charge as presenter of this final masque, Prospero allays the concomitant regrets and anxieties which the strangeness and happiness of this ending might entail. When

Alonso agrees to the marriage of Ferdinand and Miranda with some pain ('I am hers: / But, O, how oddly will it sound that I / Must ask my child forgiveness!'—196-8), he interrupts:

> There, sir, stop:
> Let us not burthen our remembrance' with
> A heaviness that's gone.   (198-200)

And later, after the Boatswain's account of the mysterious preservation of the ship and crew, Prospero consoles Alonso in his effort to understand the 'strange maze' and his desire for an oracle, just as he had attempted to allay the 'beating' of Miranda's mind in Act I and to still his own 'beating mind' in Act IV:

> Sir, my liege,
> Do not infest your mind with beating on
> The strangeness of this business; at pick'd leisure
> Which shall be shortly single, I'll resolve you,
> Which to you shall seem probable, of every
> These happen'd accidents; till when, be cheerful,
> And think of each thing well.   (245-51)

His old testiness is heard again only in his introduction of the comic conspirators:

> These three have robb'd me; and this demi-devil—
> For he's a bastard one—had plotted with them
> To take my life. Two of these fellows you
> Must know and own; this thing of darkness I
> Acknowledge mine.   (272-6)

But the other characters are moved to laughter by the appearance and the drunkenness of the three, and even Antonio is at last enough himself to speak again—a characteristically cynical witticism.

Caliban is struck by the appearance of all the courtiers as well as by that of Prospero now costumed as a Duke:

> O Setebos, these be brave spirits indeed!
> How fine my master is! I am afraid
> He will chastise me.   (261-3)

> I shall be pinch'd to death.   (276)

He is afraid, but his fear seems to have in it no trace of his former anger or malice. The final internal action of the play is Caliban's, and it is clarified by the contrasting responses of Trinculo and Stephano. The latter are not afraid at the sight of the nobility nor are they at all repentant for what they have done or intended to do. They are simply drunk and lamenting their physical hurts. When Prospero asks Stephano, 'You 'ld be King o' the isle, sirrah?' Stephano answers accurately, 'I should have been a sore one, then' (287-8). After all, the two have little to regret except a drunken dream. Like Sebastian, they were only moved to dream by the instigation of another, and they have made little imaginative commitment (only something closer to make-believe or conscious play-acting) to the dream and the actual violence—and death—its acting out would entail. But Caliban, like Antonio, has truly been committed to the dream—or, perhaps, even possessed by it. In addressing Caliban as the leader of his group of conspirators, Prospero expresses, along with his residual anger, a precise ritual of action as a condition for pardon:

> He is as disproportion'd in his manners
> As in his shape. Go, sirrah, to my cell;
> Take with you your companions; as you look
> To have my pardon, trim it handsomely.
>
> (290-3)

The ritual implies that the conspirators have relinquished whatever plans or emotions might interfere with a joyful celebration. Unlike Antonio, Caliban answers Prospero, and his statement of repentance, recognition, and determination to begin a new life is as full as Alonso's:

> Ay, that I will; and I'll be wise hereafter,
> And seek for grace. What a thrice-double ass
> Was I, to take this drunkard for a god,
> And worship this dull fool!   (294-7)

With his final speech, Caliban's moral and intellectual stature is clearly seen to be superior to Stephano's and Trinculo's. Whatever his future, it will not be merely that of a demi-devil, a villain, a drunkard, or a fool. Caliban joins Prospero and Alonso as one of the three characters in the play who show a change or resolution of character as a result of substantial conflict.

After Caliban's speech, Prospero has lost his last true servant. At the end of the play he is without special supernatural or even natural powers; he has only the strength of an older man who has already passed on the chief responsibility for the future to the next generation. Instead of attempting to create or guarantee 'providence', he is himself dependent on it—and on the prayers of his fellow sinners. Through his action, however, all the characters have been, in some sense, purged by the 'tempest' of the play. If at the end Prospero is without power and servants, he is also without anger. He has fulfilled his dream.

INDEX

Where a whole chapter is devoted to a play, the inclusive page-numbers are given in italics.